CHALLENGING CAREERS IN THE LIBRARY WORLD

In the world of tomorrow, a flood of new knowledge and innovations will make the library a more important tool than ever in the educational process. Librarians will be vitally engaged in meeting technological and social challenges and the choices of career opportunities are limitless. A stimulating look at the library world today and tomorrow and the opportunities for a rich and rewarding future for both men and women.

BOOKS BY VANYA OAKES

White Man's Folly
The Bamboo Gate
By Sun and Star
Willy Wong: American
Roy Sato: New Neighbor
Footprints of the Dragon
Desert Harvest
Hawaiian Treasure
Island of Flame

Challenging Careers in the Library World

by

VANYA OAKES

Virginia Armstrong Oakes.

photographs

JULIAN MESSNER NEW YORK

Printed in the United States of America

ISBN 0-671-32300-8 Cloth Trade
0-671-32301-6 MCE

Library of Congress Catalog Card No. 70-123173

To
Louis Lasco

ACKNOWLEDGMENTS

To mention all the librarians who have contributed some morsel of information, some pertinent comment that now finds its way into this book would be an impossibility. I do, however, wish to express my gratitude to those unidentified librarians whom I have taken the liberty of quoting; in most cases, the passage appeared in a source included in the chapter bibliography. My gratitude also to the special librarians who took time from busy schedules to show me their collections.

Librarians have not been the only contributors. Herewith a word of thanks to those who shelve books, the clerical staffs who man the circulation desks, the versatile library assistants—without them there would be no libraries and no book.

And last, but certainly not least, I am indebted to several young adult users of the Hollywood Regional Library for their comments and suggestions.

CONTENTS

I THE LIBRARY TODAY 9

II THE LIBRARY AND TECHNOLOGICAL CHANGE 19

III THE LIBRARY AND SOCIAL CHANGE 35

IV THE PUBLIC LIBRARY 52
City and County
Adults
Children
Young People

V THE PUBLIC LIBRARY 71
City and County
Audiovisual
Bookmobiles
Behind the Scenes

VI THE PUBLIC LIBRARY 91
Federal and State

VII SPECIAL LIBRARIES 112

VIII LIBRARIES ON CAMPUS 127

IX SCHOOL LIBRARIES 138

X PREPARATION FOR A PROFESSION 149

XI IF YOU'RE NOT A LIBRARIAN 163

XII OCCUPATIONAL OUTLOOK 173

ACCREDITED LIBRARY SCHOOLS 182

INDEX 187

I

THE LIBRARY TODAY

*"In today's world, with its wealth of new
information, its heightened speed, and its
widened horizons, the professional librarian's
role is truly one of great importance."*

The Royal Bank of Canada
Monthly Letter, May, 1969

WHAT IS A LIBRARIAN?

According to one abridged dictionary a librarian is: (1) a
person in charge of a library or a part of a library; (2) a
person trained for work in a library. Webster's *Collegiate
Dictionary* defines a librarian as a specialist in the care or
management of a library. And Webster's *Unabridged
Dictionary* adds: one whose special task is the management of any body of literature (musical scores for an or-
chestra, for example).

Any or all of these definitions are accurate—as far as
they go. But they are incomplete, for not one of them
mentions service to a public. And this—the desire to serve
others—is the most important characteristic of a good librarian. Whether in a public library, in a school or on a
college campus, in government or industry, in an art
museum or an audiovisual center—the librarian helps
people. Fundamentally he is a go-between, a mediator
between the library user and what he needs to know for

9

work or study, or what he wants for his leisure hours. Above all else, therefore, the good librarian is people-oriented. Or in the words of the 1968 National Advisory Commission on Libraries:

> *"The librarian of today and tomorrow must have many technical and professional skills, but above all else he must have skill with people."*

WHAT IS A LIBRARY?

Again, according to the dictionaries, a library is: (1) a collection of books; (2) a room or building where a collection of books is kept; (3) a place where a collection of books, etc., is kept for reading or reference; (4) a place in which books, manuscripts, musical scores or other literary or artistic materials are kept for use but not for sale.

What is the key word in these definitions? *Kept*—reflecting the out-of-date image of the library as a storage place.

$$\text{Storage} = \text{Static} = \text{Past}$$
$$\text{Use} \quad = \text{Active} = \text{Present}$$

Today's library—large or small, publicly or privately supported—resembles a bank more than a warehouse.

Bank	*Library*
1. contains savings accumulated over a long period	contains recorded knowledge and experience accumulated over a long period

2. keeps a part of its reserves available so that cash can be obtained on demand or short notice

keeps information and materials easily available to meet requests

3. remaining assets require the assistance of a specialist

assistance of a reference librarian required to locate information or materials not easily found

A library, then, exists to be used. And the librarian is there to help the user.

WHAT, EXACTLY, DOES A LIBRARIAN DO?

Here is what one librarian, who is both a reference and a young adult librarian, does. What follows is the *duties description* section of a job classification survey. In this case the duties described are for the Hollywood Regional Branch of the Los Angeles Public Library system, a large branch with ten smaller ones attached to it.

Service to the Public

I answer questions for patrons, at the reference desk and over the telephone, and direct them to sources of information. I act as a reader's adviser when requested. *While on Duty:* I read professional literature. I select material for the information file. I file and discard material for business services. I revise the selection of material for the pamphlet file. I check patron requests for magazines & postal reserves.

Workroom Duties

I make the weekly and daily desk schedules for the librarians, and assign substitutions in community branches as required. I revise the biweekly time sheets. I file cards in the catalog for new books, and withdraw them for books no longer in the collection. I fill book racks for patron inspection. I check the shelves against the list of books on reserve to see if any have slipped past the clerks.

Service to Young Adults

I plan and organize the program for this group, with its special requirements and interests. I answer students' questions and act as readers' adviser for recreational reading. I conduct school groups on introductory tours of the library. I visit school librarians, to explain what library services are available and are of particular interest to students. I plan and mount displays on the young adult bulletin board. I write news releases for school newspapers. I plan special programs.

I attend young adult meetings, and serve on committees as assigned. I submit monthly and annual reports. I read professional literature. I maintain records and files of pertinent material, such as book lists.

Book Collection

I submit a book budget and plan distribution of allocated funds. I maintain a book fund expenditure work sheet. I check order sheets for new books and for branch holdings and needs. I inspect new books at the central library. I discuss the selection of new books with the senior librarian and prepare the order sheet. I indicate on the shelf list which books are in the young adult collection. I replace books missing or needed in all subject categories; for this purpose I maintain a suggestion file, to which the staff contributes. I check the replacement order sheets for branch holdings and make a tentative selection. I confer with the senior librarian and submit the completed order sheet to her. I read and review books for evaluation meetings, at which time it is decided which books are to be kept in the collection. I read as many books in the young adult collection as time permits.

I supervise the section in the public area allocated to the young adult collection. I add to and withdraw from this collection on a continuing basis. I make the necessary changes on the shelf list as books are withdrawn or shelved with the adult collection. I inspect the collection for volumes in need of rebinding.

Adult Book Collection

I select titles to be replaced in an assigned section of the collection (social sciences). I check the branch shelf list and the central library department replacement sheets for branch holdings. I check three sources for other required information. I type the order forms or prepare the replacement order sheets.

I examine new books at the central library for the assigned section. I recommend which books shall be added to the collection. I examine all new books received in the branch.

I inspect the shelves in three sections of the collection and withdraw books no longer needed or in bad condition.

Substitutions

I substitute in the children's room and in community branches as needed.

Public Relations

I speak to community groups as time permits. I write news releases for special occasions.

Supervision

I am in charge of the branch when the senior librarian is not on the premises. I assume other supervisory responsibilities as assigned.

The duties at Hollywood resemble those of an average medium-size library, either a branch in a large system or the largest unit in a smaller one. The duties vary, depending on whether you work in a branch or in a department of a large library and whether you are an adult, young adult or children's librarian. They vary, too, in other types of libraries—school, college or university, special or audiovisual. No matter what the size or type of library, however, one thing remains the same—the division between the work with the public and the behind-the-scenes activities, without which no library could serve its public.

HOW TO CHOOSE A CAREER

Don't become a victim of statistics.

All too often the analysis of possible occupations consists of collecting statistics—salaries, hours, vacations and fringe benefits, future demand. On the basis of such facts and figures, you may or you may not decide on a career that suits *you*.

Do analyze yourself—first.

Start a notebook, and from time to time jot down answers to three questions:

> What do you want to do?
> What do you want to have?
> What do you want to be?

After several weeks, or months, there will emerge a profile of *you*. Also, while you are getting to know yourself, browse through the many career books and pamphlets available through your library. Then, using the same questions, think about them in relation to whatever occupations interest you most. Take library service and information science, for example.

What do you want to do?

1. Do you want to work with people? If so, which age group—children, young adults, adults or all three?
2. Do you want to be a specialist, in a large public library or in a smaller and highly specialized company library, or do you prefer being a generalist who handles all subjects in less depth?
3. Do you want to work behind the scenes, in one of the technical services? Are you interested in work connected with the computer and/or data processing?

What do you want to have?

1. Security even if it means stagnation? A large bank account? Security without stagnation?

2. Opportunity for advancement?
3. Adventure?

What do you want to be? What kind of person do you want to be?

1. Do you want to serve others, or do you thrive on competition?
2. Do you want to work in an organization which regards people as commodities, or do you prefer a working life which connects you with your fellow-man?
3. Do you want to be part of a big business or government organization, or are you happier being more your own boss in a smaller one?

These are not merely theoretical or philosophical questions. The answers to them will determine the type and size of library you choose, the library school you will attend, and your undergraduate preparation.

Once you have a clearer picture of yourself, and of your place in the career of your choice, then collect the statistics. Check the *Occupational Outlook Handbook,* a Department of Labor publication which is updated every two years and which is available in almost any library. In it you will find information about the training needed, the opportunity for advancement, the employment outlook and earning and working conditions.

The figures will, of course, vary from year to year. But, where library service and information science is concerned, one thing is unlikely to change for years to come. The demand for professional librarians, for trained specialists in information science, exceeds the supply.

This, in turn, means that you will have freedom of

choice—*if* you plan carefully. You can work where you wish: north or south, east or west, at home or abroad. You can work with the age group you enjoy the most. You can work in the type of library which most interests you.

As you read about the many types of libraries, keep in mind the difference between a generalist and a specialist. This is not a new development. There have always been subject specialists and librarians who supply information about many subjects but in less depth. Since World War II and the information explosion, however, the need for more subject specialists has steadily increased. So it is more important than ever to keep this distinction in mind when preparing for a library career.

A CAREER IN THIS CHANGING WORLD

Change is one of the few certainties in today's world. Formerly, most people chose a career and it became a lifetime occupation. Today this is no longer true. As a 1966 Labor Department report pointed out: "Today's worker can anticipate at least three different careers in his lifetime, so rapid is technological change."

Change—sometimes rapid, sometimes halting—is widespread in the library world of today. But so varied are the functions of libraries, so challenging the problems and prospects facing them, that you can change—and grow—within the field.

What librarians do now and may be doing in the future, what exciting and rewarding opportunities are available in the various kinds of libraries—these are subjects to be explored in detail. But first a look at today's rapidly changing world, for the field of library service and information science cannot be understood without understanding how and why it is being affected by these changes.

We take for granted that we live in a world that is changing with dizzying speed. We take for granted, that is, the spectacular changes in science and technology. Less spectacular because less publicized, but as far-reaching, are other explosive changes. John W. Gardner, former Secretary of Health, Education and Welfare, says: "Our status quo has been knocked head over heels by the revolutions in science and technology, in transportation, in communication and the processing of information, in industry, agriculture and education, in demography and biomedical affairs. . . ."

Put them all together and the result is a social and cultural revolution, a revolution which affects society as a whole as well as individual communities—and therefore libraries. A library can exist only as a segment of society, in some particular community. Libraries, in fact, are on the front line of the information and technological, the sociological and cultural revolutions of our time.

II

THE LIBRARY AND
TECHNOLOGICAL CHANGE

In the 16th century, when the poet Edmund Spenser
wrote about "These ever whirling wheels of change," the
wheels whirled steadily but very slowly. By the middle
of the 20th century, they were whirling frantically and at
computer speed.

The 1950s and the 1960s were the decades of the "ex-
plosions."

Information: knowledge increased geometrically.

Population: the number of people on earth zoomed
astronomically.

Technology: the age of electronics and the computer arrived.

Singly and collectively, these far-reaching changes have
had and will continue to have a volcanic impact upon the
library world.

INFORMATION

From the time of Christ to the year 1750 all of knowledge
doubled. After that it took only 150 years to double again,

and after that only 50 years. Which brings us to 1950. By 1960—a mere ten years later—all of knowledge had once more doubled. And in 1968 experts estimated that knowledge had again doubled.

Coupled with this over-all growth of knowledge is the information explosion. Startling statistic: every 24 hours enough information is published to fill seven sets of encyclopedias. Other startling statistics: every 60 seconds more than 2,000 pages of books, newspapers and other printed matter are published in some part of the world. And it is estimated that some 320,000 books are published annually throughout the world. In addition, more than 33,000 newspapers and 70,000 periodicals come off the presses—not to mention almost 100,000 scientific and technical journals, in more than 60 languages, with two new ones added each day.

In the United States, in 1967 there were 21,877 new books and 6,885 new editions of older ones. In 1964 the figures were: 20,542 new books and 7,909 new editions—nearly twice as many as in 1960.

One long-range study showed that printed materials in major college and university libraries have been doubling every sixteen years. Should this trend continue, by the year 2040 the library at Yale, for example, would have accumulated some 200,000,000 volumes. Eight acres of floor space would be needed to house more than 6,000 miles of shelves and some 750,000 drawers of catalog cards. Furthermore, the report estimated, new material would be arriving at the doors at the rate of 12,000,000 annually. Getting this material ready so that it could be found and used would require 6,000 additional catalogers.

Also arriving daily are pamphlets and reports, United Nations publications and government documents (national, state, municipal and foreign). To these must be added the ever-increasing quantity of nonprint materials —maps and music, films and filmstrips, records and tapes.

The awesome magnitude of the information explosion is dramatically illustrated by the size of the new U.S. Printing Office—it covers 40 acres, six more than the Pentagon. The information explosion might perhaps more accurately be called a deluge—a deluge that threatens to bury libraries, but at the same time make more knowledge available to more people than ever before in history.

POPULATION

Like the weather, everyone talks about the population explosion while viewers with alarm cite frightening statistics. But, unlike the weather, societies throughout the world are trying to do something about it. With what success, we will know only at some future and unpredictable date.

What we do know now is that the world's population doubled first around 1650. By 1850 it had doubled again; and by 1930 it had doubled once more. The 1960 census placed the U.S. population at somewhat more than 180,-000,000. By 1967 it had reached the 200,000,000 mark.

What we think we know is that by 1975 the world's population will have doubled again. And by 1980 there will be 250,000,000 people living in the United States.

As far as libraries are concerned, however, the significant statistics are those concerning education:

	1960	1966	per cent increase
High school degrees	10,249,000	13,364,000	30.4
College degrees	3,570,000	6,085,000	70.4

Before long, it is estimated, there will be 20,000,000 young college graduates in the United States. And today 90 per cent of all college graduates are settling in metropolitan areas.

What these figures mean is that an ever-increasing part of the population is accustomed to using libraries to get information, and that a certain percentage—not yet predictable—will continue to do so. In addition, nearly everyone preparing for or already working in a white-collar job uses the library at one time or another. One distraught secretary said, "I'm always being sent to look things up."

In other words, more and more people are needing more and more information. How do we bring the two together? How do we close the knowledge gap? We *must* close it if American society is to survive. And this, basically, is the difficult and exciting task ahead, for the library world and for the individual librarian.

TECHNOLOGY

Herman Hollerith is credited with inventing the punched card, the foundation stone of automation. In his autobiography Mr. Hollerith comments: "I was having tea with Dr. B. one day, and he told me that there ought to be a machine for doing the purely mechanical work of totaling population and other statistics."

Dr. B., it turns out, was one Dr. John Shaw Billings. In 1880, at the time of the tea, he was the Army Surgeon General's librarian (he later became the director of the New York Public Library).

Fifty years later, a young librarian at the University of Texas asked for a grant to study the application of the punched-card machine to the problems of checking books in and out. He received the generous sum of $300, together with the admonition that he spend it wisely.

In the decades since 1930 many other librarians and library systems have experimented with various machines, trying to find those suitable for library operations. Until recently most of these experiments have concentrated on what might be called housekeeping functions: checking materials in and out (in library lingo, circulation), ordering of materials (acquisition) and keeping records of magazines, government documents and the like (serial records control).

In the words of one librarian: "The problem is one of learning what it is that we want the machines to do and then designing machines and the appropriate software that can do it efficiently."

Storage and Retrieval

With the information explosion these inseparable problems of the library world became a full-fledged crisis. How to store the mountains of material? How to extract the information for the user when he needs it?

Over the centuries the printed page has been the medium of storage, for both fact and fiction. Fortunately, by the time the paper deluge descended upon libraries, photography had come of age and miniaturization was developing. Today libraries have begun to utilize various techniques to solve the storage problem.

Miniaturization techniques, past and pending, are important to libraries, now and in the future. But it is the computer that is catapulting the library into the machine age—especially the third-generation computer, capable of storing up to 8,000,000 items of data. Miniaturization and/or computers can control the storage problem. The principal problem, now and in the foreseeable future, is not storage but retrieval—the finding of material. For of what value is a magnificent collection across the street from where you live or work or study if you cannot get at the material quickly and efficiently?

Because the computer both stores and retrieves at lightning speed, it is rapidly becoming the key tool in library operations. The third-generation computer processes data in millionths of a second. The speed of the fourth-generation computer—ready for the public before 1980—will be measured in nanoseconds. What is a nanosecond? It is to a second as a second is to 30 years—almost unimaginable, the tiniest sliver of time. As Quincy Mumford, former librarian of the Library of Congress, pointed out: "The computer is fast becoming as essential in today's library as the time-hallowed card catalogue was in yesterday's."

As of 1967 only a small number of libraries in the United States—about 3 per cent—were using data-processing equipment. Although focused mainly on technical processes and circulation control, data processing is beginning to be used for indexing and bibliographic work. The National Library of Medicine, for example, is nearing the push-button stage. MEDLARS—Medical Literature

Analysis and Retrieval System—is a computer-based operation that stores, analyzes and retrieves bibliographic information for physicians and medical researchers. In addition, it prepares the *Index Medicus* and other bibliographies for publication.

Systems of Cooperation

MEDLARS has designated five search centers, in various parts of the country, to provide bibliographic services: Harvard University, the University of Alabama, the University of Michigan, the University of Colorado and the University of California at Los Angeles. Linked to these centers will be eleven regional medical libraries. U.C.L.A., for example, is the Pacific Southwest Medical Library serving medical institutions and personnel throughout the four-state area of Arizona, California, Nevada and Hawaii. Such regional libraries serve as intermediate links between local medical libraries and the National Library of Medicine, to form a nationwide network.

Suppose, for example, that a surgeon in Tucson, Ariz., needs a certain article on a certain type of heart defect. His own hospital library does not have the journal, nor do any of the larger medical libraries in Arizona. The librarian would then send the request to U.C.L.A by teletype, telegram, telephone or airmail—depending on the facilities available and the urgency of the case. Should U.C.L.A. not have the journal, the surgeon would be notified immediately and his request forwarded by teletype to the National Library of Medicine.

Although it will be a long time before you can be hooked into a similar system, there is emerging a pattern of interlibrary cooperation aimed at getting accurate information to people who need it, wherever they are.

For some time it has been possible to have materials sent to your neighborhood library, if you live in a metropolitan or county area with a large system. Using the Inter Library Loan (I.L.L.) procedure, you fill out a request at your local library. If the system has a larger regional branch, it goes there first. Should what you want not be in that collection, it then goes to the main library—along with all the other requests from all the other branches. All this takes time, especially if the main library owns the item but is out of it. So while your request wanders, you wait—with the deadline for that term paper looming ever closer.

If the collection in the main library cannot fill the request, it may be forwarded to another system or to the state library. For the serious researcher, a university will be contacted and, if all else fails, the Library of Congress. In the past, all this has been done by mail. And while your request continues to wander, you wait and wait.

If the volume or information is not needed in a hurry, the I.L.L. procedure provides an excellent service. But for the serious student or the busy businessman, both with deadlines to meet, it has obvious limitations. And what about people in rural areas? The farmer or rancher may have urgent need for information about pesticides.

Librarians have long been aware of these limitations, but with the tools available it was the best that could be done. Now, however, with the advent of the computer and electronic breakthroughs, the library world stands on the threshold of an exciting era.

The basic philosophy on which to build already exists. To cite one example, in 1967 California issued a master plan for the development of public library service in the state, the basic principles of which are:

1. Every citizen of California has an equal right of access to all of the knowledge resources of the state.
2. The potential library needs of the individual are equally great, urgent and complex, whether the citizen lives in a remote hamlet or in the heart of a metropolitan area; therefore, the place of residence cannot be a factor which limits or determines how much and what kind of library service the individual is to receive.
3. In spite of the mobility of today's public, the individual cannot be expected to move from place to place in his quest for material; rather it is the responsibility of the library to provide unlimited access through whatever point of contact the borrower finds convenient.

Stripped of legalistic jargon, this means that a library —any library—should see to it that everyone gets what he needs, when and where he needs it. And many other states and areas have prepared similar statements of goals.

This is the theory. What about practice? Note those two key words *"unlimited* access." Libraries are still a long distance from that goal, but they are moving along the road toward it.

In California several cooperative systems are already in operation, the blueprint for blanketing the entire state in existence. In such a network, smaller individual libraries or systems are linked to a larger one. For example, the Inland Library System, with San Bernardino the mother unit, spreads out over an area of 20,000 square miles, and consists of six separate libraries serving some

700,000 people. To put it another way, any one of those 700,000 readers now has access to over 1,500,000 volumes, rather than being limited to the average 200,000 in his own library.

Further south, SCAN—Southern California Answering Network—serves three areas: Los Angeles, Pasadena and Santa Barbara. What cannot be answered elsewhere is funneled to headquarters in the main research library of the Los Angeles Public Library.

What kind of questions does SCAN tackle? In a 1965 Christmas speech Adlai Stevenson quoted a phrase "remember what peace there may be in silence." A patron attributed it to Desirata Manehram, believed to be a medieval monk. As it turned out, it was an excerpt from a poem "Desiderata," by Max Ehrmann, who died in 1948.

When a group of Indians landed on Alcatraz Island in San Francisco Bay, a writer wanted to know if there was a legal basis for such action. The SCAN staff tracked down article 6, paragraph 4 of an 1868 Sioux Treaty which stated: "Male Indians over the age of 18 can reside or occupy any reservation or territory for which the U.S. Government has no specified purpose other than an Indian reservation."

A housewife wanted to know what to do about some mildewed oak furniture. No reference to treating oak was found, but information about wood in general was provided.

The development of rapid communications has made such networks possible, with the teletype linking the separate libraries to each other and to the state library. The electronic breakthrough has also made possible a dramatic new development in library service—facsimile transmission. Using electronic signals carried by telephone circuits, the exchange of reference materials between libraries can now be accomplished in a matter of minutes.

Facsimile transmission consists of a photosensitive light cell attached to a revolving drum. It scans a given page of print and transmits the electric impulses over the telephone. At the other end there is a receiving unit, with a standard 8½ × 11-inch page. The transmission time is five or six minutes. In effect, the process provides any patron within a certain area with access to the materials and professional services of a major metropolitan library.

At the Bay Area Reference Center in San Francisco, for example, a request was received for a specific article on mental retardation. The librarian got the magazine, made a copy of the article and sent it via facsimile transmission to the library some 20 miles to the north. Total time: half an hour.

Across the country, in New York, there are nine reference and research library systems operating under the Reference and Research Library Resources program. The Three Rs program, as it is called, aims to provide better and quicker access to in-depth materials for the serious library user—college students and faculty, professional people, business and industry and government at all levels. These networks tie together several public libraries, a number of college and university ones and libraries with highly specialized collections.

On a national scale the Library of Congress undertook to assess the long-term value of automation for libraries. A detailed study came to the conclusion that it was not yet practical to retrieve the content of books by computer in large research libraries. For, unlike specialized medical or technical collections, these libraries cover an almost limitless number of subjects. The study did conclude, however, that in several areas of library work automation could speed up processes and provide greater access to materials.

As a result, in 1966 the Library of Congress launched a pilot project in which 16 libraries, of different types and in various parts of the country, participated. MARC—Machine Readable Catalog Data—distributed magnetic tapes containing catalog information, the kind of information you find in the catalog of your local library. MARC records were used in various experiments, such as the production of a book catalog and the use of computer-printed cards.

The Library of Congress is also working in the field of bibliographic information. Today in its 16 reading rooms, and in other large research libraries, the user must consult card or book catalogs to ferret out the information he needs—a tedious and time-consuming task. Tomorrow he will ask the librarian to query a computer which, in a matter of minutes, will provide sources of information on a specific subject. But a word of caution: "tomorrow" may be quite far in the future. There are many problems yet to be solved before computer-based services are really useful on a large scale. They are difficult problems but challenging ones—problems which librarians entering the field will tackle.

One of these problems has been, and doubtless will continue to be, money. Obviously, all of these recent developments and experiments have cost a great deal. Where did the money come from?

In large part, it came from the Federal Government, without whose financial assistance most of the forward-looking projects would still be stuck on the drawing boards. By 1969 there were six major laws on the books with library-related sections.

1. Library Services and Construction Act.
   This provides for, among other things, development of interlibrary cooperation.
2. Elementary and Secondary Education Act.
   Title II concerns school library resources (textbooks and other instructional materials).
3. Higher Education Act.
4. Higher Education Facilities Act.
   Federal funds have strengthened college and university libraries in every state of the union.
5. Medical Library Assistance Act.
6. National Defense Education Act.
   This provides for summer institutes for school librarians, and awards graduate fellowships.

Although these are now the laws of the land, they can be repealed or amended. And, of course, Congress must annually appropriate the money. Because of this, the library world is very active in the Washington arena these days, with the American Library Association and other concerned organizations lobbying vigorously.

WHAT OF THE FUTURE?

From whatever source, large sums of money will be needed to bring together the library and the computer, the printed page and the electronic image, to develop the emerging information networks. There is already a growing realization that we must spend such sums in at least one area of the information explosion—science and technology. If we do not, we may lose control of it—with disastrous results for the nation. As one library school dean put it: "The computers won't save us money, but they may save us."

Mechanization, automation—computers and data processing. Will the librarian of the future have to be a technologist or a technician? A mathematician or a statistician? A robot pushing buttons?

There is no need to push the panic button. How many of us can fix the transmission in our cars or install new brakes? Yet we drive cars. When automobiles were new, a driver did need to be something of a mechanic, for at any moment he might have "to get out and get under." But today specialists attend to the automobile's ills.

So, too, in the field of information science, where the body of specialists is growing. We as librarians need to know how to use the new tools—not how to construct or program or repair them. We need only enough understanding of the new tools to acquire the skill to operate them—the same sort of skill we must have to operate an automobile or a dishwasher.

Above all, we need an open mind about their potential value to the information seeker. Without that we cannot serve as the mediator between these new tools and the needs of the user.

A college dean has aptly summarized the situation facing the library world in the decade ahead: "At one end of the historical spectrum, a slave carrying a message in a clay tablet; at the other a computerized push-button library. Today, after nearly 3,000 years of development, the library is just now entering the machine age, and possibilities are so cloudy and complex that no one can say with assurance how far the mechanization or automation of the library will travel in the foreseeable future."

However "cloudy and complex," there is a growing realization that access to information has become crucial to the health and welfare, security and continued progress of the United States and the world.

The crisis in information and library science is critical. But what is a crisis? The Chinese character for the word joins the characters for danger and opportunity. There may be a danger. But there is also the opportunity to provide man with the information he needs to grapple with problems that have beset him for centuries—*if* he can get at that information. To help him get that information has become the mission of the librarian.

FOR MORE INFORMATION

Collier's Encyclopedia
  Each edition also includes articles on libraries. 1968, vol. 14:597-599. *Documentation.*
Encyclopedia Americana
  Each edition contains an up-to-date article on libraries. 1967, vol. 17:397-400. New Technology.
Encyclopedia of Social Sciences. 1968, vol. 7:314-337.
  Information Storage and Retrieval: Information Sci-

ences. Detailed analysis of the problems and prospects.

World Book. 1969, vol. 12:213-233.

Over-all survey of library world, past and present.

American Library Association. "Library Automation: Tomorrow Becomes Today," A. L. A. *Bulletin,* June, 1967.

Several articles comprise this special section; includes bibliography.

Shera, Jesse H. "Librarians against Machines," *Science,* May 12, 1967.

Need of a professional philosophy if librarians are to adopt and adapt the new technology.

Encyclopedia of Library and Information Science. New York: Marcel Dekka, Inc., 1968, vol. I.

III

THE LIBRARY AND
SOCIAL CHANGE

What is the social responsibility of libraries? How can they meet the urgent social crises of our time? How can they become an active, constructive force for social change?

These are questions which the library world is trying to answer. Administrators and librarians on bookmobiles, at professional meetings and in day-to-day activities—they are all wrestling with the social problems of our time.

This is today. What of yesterday? What has been the role of the library—the public library in particular—in the past? What kind of public has it served?

The Past

During colonial times there were few public libraries. In the Southern settlements there were some "parish" libraries, a concept brought to America by a Reverend Thomas Bray, who planned to organize parochial libraries in England and America. In 1713 another English minister donated 124 volumes to New York for the establishment of a public library.

In 1730 Benjamin Franklin wrote to a member of the Junto, a debating club composed mostly of young artisans and tradesmen, concerning the need for books. By "clubbing our books to a common library," he suggested, each member would have "the advantage of using the books of all the other members, which would be nearly as beneficial as if each owned the whole."

The plan was to keep the books in the room used for meetings, making them available to all the members. For some reason, this arrangement did not work satisfactorily, and Franklin then advanced a plan for a subscription library. Each member bought a share in the common property (cost: 40 shillings) and paid an annual fee. And so began the Library Company of Philadelphia, whose directors held their first meeting in November of 1731. During the remaining colonial years, other communities organized similar subscription libraries.

The Revolution interrupted the growth of libraries and nearly destroyed the one in New York. Later, as the self-governing commonwealths were created and a central government emerged, emphasis on reading gained momentum. How else, reasoned our forefathers, could citizens acquire the learning necessary for sound judgment on matters crucial to the survival and growth of the republic? Legislators, too, required learning for sound judgment. And so the Library of Congress came into existence, in 1800, to be followed by similar collections for the use of state legislatures.

The subscription libraries, with their scholarly collections and high fees, were available only to the well-to-do. But by the 1820s the results of the Industrial Revolution had reached the marketplace, bringing more people to the industrial centers—people with little money and limited education.

To meet their needs, a new type of library made its appearance. In 1820 the Mechanics' Apprentices Library of Boston was founded, to be followed by similar institutions all over the United States. A reader paid to belong to these libraries, too, but the fees were modest: in Cincinnati, for example, members paid $3 a year, ladies and minors 50¢. The books provided were those needed by artisans, apprentices and their families for "instruction, edification and recreation."

About the same time, mercantile libraries were organized, for the benefit of "merchants' clerks"—the forerunners of today's white-collar workers. Their objectives paralleled those of the mechanics' libraries, but they served readers with slightly higher incomes and vastly higher social ambitions.

Having served the public of their era, the various subscription libraries dwindled in number, went out of existence or were absorbed by the public library movement. Even today, however, a few remain—among them, one in San Francisco at the Mechanics Institute and the Boston Athenaeum.

The subscription libraries served people of similar interests, income and social level, not a broad, general public. And, in most cases, the members provided all of the funds. As the standard of living slowly rose and popular education spread, the public library movement began to develop. It aimed to provide a storehouse of books which would be free to call citizens of a community, and which would be financed by tax-supported funds. The underlying philosophy conceived of libraries as giving the citizen an opportunity to gain useful knowledge and thereby advance his station in life. If such an opportunity were not provided, it was feared, many a worthy citizen would be "otherwise doomed to obscurity by poverty."

The public library might even be useful in the battle against crime. The city levied taxes to punish crime; why should it not do the same to prevent crime? As the directors of one Massachusetts library pleaded in petitioning the city council for a free public library: "Let the library be free to all, and then, perhaps, there will be one young man less in a place where intoxicating drinks are found. . . . Make the library free to all, and then, perhaps, there will be one young woman less to fall from the path of purity and goodness down to that depth of degradation and misery to which only a woman can fall."

In 1833 in Peterborough, New Hampshire, a free town library supported by a municipal tax opened its doors. In 1848 the Massachusetts legislature passed an act authorizing a tax-supported public library in Boston. When that city's board of aldermen later voted to accept this statute, it became the first law to ratify the establishment and maintenance of a public library as a municipal institution supported by taxation. And the public library as we know it today was officially born.

The public library was born, but not housed. Many collections occupied out-of-the-way corners in the local city hall or were tucked away in some most unusual locations—a millinery shop, the balcony of a drugstore, a doctor's reception hall, a room in an opera house, some vacant space over a meat market or the building providing shelter for the horses of a fire department.

To the rescue came Scotland-born Andrew Carnegie, the Steel King, who earmarked most of his enormous fortune for "the improvement of mankind." His philanthropies ranged from the establishment of the Carnegie Institutes in Pittsburgh and the Carnegie Endowment for International Peace to the invention of the Simplified Spelling Board, the installation of more than 700 church organs, the construction of more than 1,600 library buildings.

Applications for the construction of suitable quarters for book collections were received by mail. Most requests included eloquent accounts of the community—the cleanliness of the streets, the number of eager school children and devout churchgoers, the dawn-to-dusk industry of the inhabitants. On the other hand, one Wisconsin mayor pointed out that a library would serve to counteract the evil influence of the town's 20 saloons. Another community in Iowa, however, boasted that it had had no saloons for 30 years—an accomplishment which certainly merited reward.

Mr. Carnegie and his private secretary examined all requests and frequently asked for additional information. One subscription library in Nebraska, for example, was asked to be more specific about $939 of "miscellaneous receipts." In addition to the fees of its 139 members and cash donations, these included:

Proceeds from the Library Hog	$86.05
(The weight of a gift hog was guessed for 25¢ a try at the county fair, with the hog going to the winner.)	
From the sale of Library Maid (a gift heifer sold at auction)	17.60
The Fourth of July Tag Sale by the ladies.	77.77

Although some requests were rejected, most communities applying received funds for a building. The city or town, for its part, had to provide a suitable site, and the local governing body had to contribute an annual sum of not less than 10 per cent of the Carnegie gift. Today these sturdy square buildings are disappearing. But the impetus Andrew Carnegie gave to the public library movement will never disappear.

The People's University

For several decades around the turn of the century, the Carnegie libraries did indeed contribute toward "the improvement of mankind." Throughout this period the public library, as well as the public schools, translated into action the American belief in education.

In those days relatively few people went on to college; in 1900, for instance, out of a total population of nearly 76,000,000 only 238,000 were enrolled in institutions of higher learning. The public library therefore became the prime source of continuing education for those whose formal learning ended with grammar or high school. Its philosophy was rooted in the conviction that reading could help the individual to grow, provided he had the will to seek out and pursue knowledge. Its objective was to make learning available to an ever-widening circle of citizens. The public library was to become the People's University.

One group of citizens it served with outstanding success were the foreign-born. By the 1880s the waves of immigrants were reaching a peak, bringing peoples from many European countries with little or no knowledge of the English language or American customs. But they did come with a yearning for knowledge, thinking of it as the first rung on the ladder to a better standard of living.

Once here, the immigrants found that libraries had organized classes in beginning English and citizenship. Gradually, collections that provided the best literature in the language of the country of origin were developed. In other words, the public library supplied not only materials to help in the process of assimilation, but leadership as well.

When the Depression of the 1930s gripped the country, the public library found itself on the horns of an insoluble dilemma. On the one hand, there were drastic cuts in its funds. On the other hand, there were pressures for more services with so many people out of work, people with nothing to do and no place to go. In most city libraries it was standing room only, as thousands of persons packed the reading rooms. Some used the opportunity to study, others to fill empty hours with recreational reading, many just to have a place to sit and, in winter, to keep warm. One observer saw the library as "a line of defense against the disappointments, the discontents, the discouragement and the despair which follow lost jobs."

In both world wars the public library was where the action was. In World War I the American Library Association organized the Library War Service Program, employing some 700 librarians; and there were Carnegie Corporation buildings on 36 large army posts. This pioneer project demonstrated the importance of books for maintaining morale among the troops, so that in World War II a much larger operation was launched. Each of the services had collections wherever troops were stationed, on ship or on shore. And, once again, the public library contributed the know-how and the librarians to mount what was—and is today—a massive operation.

The period immediately following World War II was

one of repairing and rebuilding—not only the buildings themselves, but collections and staffs. It was also a period of experimentation in leisure-time activities. Libraries provided meeting places for the *Great Books* programs and cooperated with the Ford Foundation's Fund for Adult Education. Concerned about the growing number of older citizens faced with idleness and boredom, the public library sponsored clubs with names like Golden Age, Live Long and Like It.

In addition, simmering under the surface was the beginning of the struggle to cope with the rising tide of information. And then came 1957—and Sputnik.

Startled, stunned and somewhat scared, the United States discovered that it lagged behind the U.S.S.R. in the space race. In the scramble to catch up, educators revamped courses of study, stepped up requirements and assigned non-textbook reading and research papers. Students, students and more students descended upon the public libraries of the land. Pressured by teachers and parents, they plunged into "research" in pursuit of that good grade that led to the college campus. As one harassed student put it, "Drop into the public library or drop out of school." At the peak of the near-panic, the survival of library collections and staffs were in doubt.

In due course, however, the country regained its balance and moved ahead into what has come to be called the "age of affluence." And the public library moved with it. Business and industry used it; government agencies at all levels used it; the communications media used it; and students continued to use it. Library resources had always been available to individuals or organizations if they wanted to use them; now they *had* to use them, in the struggle to keep up with the information explosion.

As for the recreational reader, he was pushed into the background but not forgotten; he could still find novels and hobby materials.

By the 1960s, in other words, the People's University had become a resource center and recreational annex for the middle class. In spite of limited finances and staff shortages, it served—and served well—the affluent society.

The Present

And then came Watts. Until one night in August of 1965 Watts—small *w*—meant units of electric power. On that night Watts—capital *W*—lit up an area of our economy, a segment of our society that was anything but affluent. The dictionary equates affluent with abundant, plentiful. But life in Watts and, it soon became apparent, other ghettos and barrios was anything but abundant and plentiful. Most people living there, in fact, were mired in poverty and hopelessness, cut off from the rest of society. Again startled and stunned, and somewhat scared, the United States was forced to realize that large chunks of the population did not share in the much-vaunted affluence.

The events of that violent summer, and the continuing turmoil in cities, caused librarians to do some serious soul-searching. At conventions and in committee meetings, they asked themselves some hard questions. Why did not more people in Watts, Harlem and elsewhere go to the library? Why did they not use it as the immigrants had in the early part of the century? Why was it not a sanctuary for the poor and oppressed, as it had been during the Depression?

James Baldwin, in *Go Tell It on the Mountain*, suggests one answer:

He loved this street not for the people or the shops but for the stone lions that guarded the great main building of the Public Library, a building filled with books and unimaginably vast, and which he had never yet dared to enter. He might, he knew, for he was a member of the branch in Harlem and was entitled to take books from any library in the city. But he had never gone in because the building was so big that it must be full of corridors and marble steps, in the maze of which he would be lost and never find the book he wanted. And then everyone, all the white people inside, would know that he was not used to great buildings, or to many books, and they would look at him with pity. . . .

The paragraph describes a black child, understandably overawed by the size and splendor of the New York library. It also describes a black child paralyzed by fear—fear of white people's reaction to him.

But what about the small community library? Shortly after the upheaval in Watts, writer Budd Schulberg started a writer's project there—a project which has since published *Fire From the Ashes: Voices of Watts*. Non-readers at first, they were interested only in self-expression. Gradually, however, as books accumulated on the pantry shelves—the first groups met in the pantry of a community house—they began to want to read.

But, almost without exception, members of this talented group refused to go into the local library. Why? Fear. Fear of anything or anyone who even remotely represented authority, the Establishment. Fear of having their addresses on record, in case of trouble. As Schulberg has pointed out, in the past libraries belonged to "the respectable." But many of those who most need libraries today are not "respectable."

Furthermore, many of them are such poor readers that a book is thought of as a hazard, not a help. For the most part, the people of the United States have considered illiteracy the problem of other countries; those 700,000,-000 adults in the world who cannot read or write are thought to be some other place. U.S. census figures indicate otherwise.

25 years of age and older	1960 census	1980 projection
Completed five to eight years of school	30,500,000	21,500,000

What these figures meant, according to sociologist Kenneth Clark, was that libraries were unusable by nonreading residents of the ghettos and barrios. The public library had become irrelevant to a large segment of our society. It sat there, waiting for people to come to it. This might have sufficed in the past, but not today. In the words of a recent American Library Association statement: "Librarians have a responsibility for reaching and serving these people now. Librarians must enlarge their knowledge of the undereducated and revise their concepts of service."

What happened when pioneering librarians did revise their concepts of service and reach out to the people who most needed help?

Venice, not many miles from downtown Los Angeles, resembles its European ancestor. It has been sinking. The sinkage, however, has been not physical but economic and psychological. Here is what a children's librarian wrote about her work in Venice.

Venice is a peculiar area. There is not one hospital, not one factory, not one housing project in the entire community. Schools and churches, with the exception of one Catholic church on the Santa Monica border, are segregated. The forty blocks of the inner ghetto consist of houses, house-front churches, little corner stores charging 75¢ for a 69¢ pound of coffee, and doing a roaring trade in candy bars, soda pop and potato chips, which for many children is a staple diet. New apartment buildings are slums even before they are occupied. Doorbell ringing is a euphemism in Venice. There are no doorbells, nor number plates nor mail slots, and as one knocks on doors, he may drive splinters into his fingers because even the wood is unfinished. . . .

The majority of non-Caucasian children have not learned to read, spell, or subtract after seven years of elementary school. The consequence is a commonly seen picture at Venice Library: tutor with tutee. U.C.L.A. had a program in progress when the Federal Project staff came to Venice. The staff embarked on one of their own. They set up a supplementary program for the long empty, summer months.

So the Federal Project Staff works with the community to defeat failure and meanwhile tries to make the library a more vivid place, something to involve the children in many aspects of living, to make them more active and competent. They listen, tape their voices, display their work, print their writings. They formed a hobby club which has been going strong for over a year. They take trips, make things, collect other things, have visits from interesting people. They have pen pals in New York, and one boy asked, "How many blocks is it to New York?" A Children's Book Jury gave awards to favorite books, story hours are accompanied by dramatic and art activities. . . .

The best customers for books are young children to whom a book is a fascinating toy without association of defeat. . . .

In another branch on the other side of sprawling Los

Angeles, a young adult librarian worked with a "teen post." Since she happened to be an actress as well as a librarian, she thought she might help with a dramatic program. To break the ice, she took along her tape recorder. Here is her report.

The kids took a long time warming up to the point where they would take a crack at hearing their voices. Some times one or two would hang around until almost closing time, before daring to put some very funny burlesque type humour on the tape. One girl, after about ten minutes of nasty, vicious jokes and nastier wisecracks, nastier than the typical teen-age banter, went soft and recorded how much the people at the teen post meant to her. She told of her insecurity and fears about herself, how they helped her against violent opposition and lack of understanding at home, how they fed her when she had been hungry, and how lost she would be without them. . . .

One young man, Mike, a former gang member who was really too old for the teen post, came in and we got him to talk into the recorder. Hesitantly at first, he talked of his feeling about the teen post and the work it was doing; how he felt it should be improved; and of his own background, which included dire poverty and a convict brother. . . .

Two weeks later one of the boys was fatally stabbed by a Negro gang. The night the boy died, Mike came to a meeting and talked the boys out of starting a feud. I have no doubt that Mike saved several lives by his talk that night. . . .

I talked to the kids individually, drawing them out. I attended their meetings at the Police Station, where they tried to make peace with a rival gang. I brought my camera and took pictures, brought prints to the kids. The idea was to do anything to help them get a feeling of "This is ME," "I am real," "I am somebody."

Adult librarians discovered that Kenneth Clark's criticism, that libraries had ceased to be relevant, was all too true. One of the basic creeds of the public library has been the right book for the right person. But for the downtrodden and undereducated person, whether in a city slum or an Indian reservation, what *is* the right book?

Once librarians got out onto the streets and into the homes of these communities, they soon found out what the people wanted. They wanted job information, literacy test materials, easy-to-read books on driving and cooking—not the classics. They wanted books on Negro history and literature in Spanish—not literary criticism and political analysis. It boiled down to the urgent need for materials in three areas—employment, education and everyday life.

In addition, librarians decided, easy-to-read materials for fun and inspiration—in very short supply in the deprived areas—were desperately needed. These include biographies of sports heroes and modern success stories, novels and hobbies.

The next problem was where to find suitable materials. Since the library was geared toward fulfilling the needs of a literate middle class, very little printed material existed for the adult with limited reading ability. Gradually, however, as Federal funds moved through the pipelines, some materials became available, much of it in pamphlet form.

Once books and pamphlets were obtainable, libraries began to develop programs tailored to the needs of their particular communities. Brooklyn, for example, launched Operation Second Chance—classes for people on welfare who wanted to become self-supporting. Cleveland worked out a Books and Jobs Program, and made lists of books for beginning adult readers. Branches in Spanish-speaking neighborhoods provided space and materials for English classes. Libraries sponsored hobby clubs and voter registration drives.

Probably the most startling, and the most disturbing, discovery for print-oriented librarians was the demand for films and records. To be sure, by the time the Federal projects took to the field, most large libraries had established audiovisual departments. But usually these non-print collections were thought of as adjuncts to books and magazines. Out in the depressed communities, the librarians found that the priority was upside down, for several obvious reasons—reading or language barriers, and the fact that the younger generation had been video kids from birth.

The imaginative librarian plunged in, learning as he went along and making do with what was at hand. Libraries rocked and rolled, held fiestas and developed programs on books and films, reading, records and recording. Film showings became commonplace—sometimes for fun, sometimes tied to a serious problem, such as drugs. Read-ins and storytelling hours included films.

The Future

In 1964 former Vice-President Hubert Humphrey wrote an article for a library journal. It began: "Next to our schools, our public libraries are potentially more important, in the 'war on poverty' than any other of our public institutions."

It concluded: "Libraries, then, can work closely with teachers and schools. They can reach out themselves, aggressively, with facilities and programs. I believe they can be powerful centers of new activity and vital stimulants to people to reach out with new hope and expectation to the world about them. Librarians can help greatly in supporting individuals in what is basically a spiritual quest. . . ."

How well has the public library done in the years since those words were written? Children's librarians have stepped up their work with schools in the disadvantaged areas, paying more visits to classrooms, having more programs in the libraries. The library has reached out to teen-agers, in or out of school, working with Teen Posts and experimenting with new programs. Librarians have searched, sometimes in vain, for materials for the under-educated adult, for the new immigrants to the cities. Although the first attempts were to reach into the Negro neighborhoods, the programs have been broadened to include Mexican-American barrios, Puerto Rican slums and Indian reservations. And today bookmobiles may be found parked at housing projects or bouncing over rutted roads toward remote reservations.

Libraries have tried hard to become "powerful centers of new activities," to bring those "vital stimulants" to the people who need them the most. The public library has done a great deal, but a great deal more remains to be done.

The social and cultural revolution of the past decade has created a library revolution. For, since the public library tries to serve all segments of society, social upheavals have a direct impact upon it.

As in the past, the library will continue to be a resource center. But it has launched programs, and is experimenting with more, to carry these resources to the people most desperately in need of them. No longer merely a reservoir of knowledge, the public library is becoming a pipeline through which information and enjoyment can flow outward. No longer limited to the privileged reader, it is out on the hustings seeking out the underprivileged citizen and using new methods to communicate with him. A University of Malaya librarian summed up the role of the library in these words: "Libraries have come to be regarded as the spearhead of new social forces attacking lethargy, ignorance and poverty. It has been recognized that economic advance stems from books just as certainly as it stems from electric power stations."

FOR MORE INFORMATION

Martin, Lowell A. "The Changes Ahead," *Library Journal,* Feb. 15, 1968. Summary of social and technological changes; problems and potentialities.

IV

THE PUBLIC LIBRARY
CITY AND COUNTY

Adults, Children, Young Adults

The Role of the Adult Librarian

One day in November of 1963 this librarian answered a telephone call at the reference desk of the Social Science Department of the Los Angeles Public Library. I could scarcely hear the woman's voice at the other end of the line, so loud was the television.

"If you can hold for just a moment," she shouted, "I'll turn the TV down."

There was a lull after she lowered the volume. The lull continued, and I murmured an automatic "Hello?"

When the lull persisted, I inquired, somewhat impatiently, "What is it, please? There are other calls. . . ."

"He's been shot," came over the phone.

"What? Who's been. . . ."

"President Kennedy—he's been shot," she repeated and hung up.

I sat there, the receiver still in my hand. The other phone rang, and the operator informed me that one party had already hung up and that another call was waiting. My paralyzed brain began to function again, and, mumbling to a colleague to take the calls, I headed for the office of the principal librarian.

For the next few hours, while it was still uncertain whether President Kennedy would live or die, we collected materials—documents concerning the presidential succession, biographies of the Kennedy family, the inaugural address and other key speeches, information on other presidential assassinations.

In the grim week that followed, we answered countless questions concerning its historic events:

> How does one address telegrams to the White House?
> How should sympathy notes to Mrs. Kennedy be phrased?
>
> What happens to the office of the Vice-Presidency?
> Who may administer the oath to the President?
>
> In what states were other presidents assassinated, or were assassination attempts made?
>
> Why was the casket kept closed?
> What is the correct way to drape the flag?
> What is the origin of the 21-gun salute?
> What is the symbolism of the riderless horse?
>
> Who may be buried in Arlington Cemetery?
> How many eternal flames are there? How are they operated?

Several years earlier the Los Angeles Public Library

had been affected by President Kennedy's nomination, with the convention in the city and Democratic headquarters in the hotel across the street from the central library. Much of the material needed by the committee drafting the platform came from the library. And both before and during the convention the communications media needed all kinds of information—biographical material, statistical data and so on.

Only rarely, of course, will most librarians find themselves so closely linked to the headlines. Usually the requests for information will be less earthshaking. But, although the day-to-day questions may not make headlines, they may be crucially important to the person needing the information. A frightened and bewildered woman had to have proof of her age for Medicare, but fire had destroyed the records in the town in which she had been born. How could she prove that she was 65 or over? A man's roof had collapsed because the landlord had left a hose running on it. How did he go about suing the errant owner? Another patron who wanted to sue was the irate lady whose wash had burned up in a laundromat. But what about those two words on the sign, "not responsible"? Did they let the owner off the hook? Material is needed to pass the citizenship test. Which is the proper governmental agency to contact about an influx of rattlesnakes?

Civic-minded citizens frequently turn to the library for information. A newly elected school board member, for example, wanted suggestions about educational magazines to which to subscribe. A woman was in search of general information on Malaysia. Soon to arrive at their home would be the 18-year-old son of a government official, an exchange student who would be living with them.

Most family-type requests for information are less exotic—how to remove stains from a certain kind of fabric, how to repair small appliances? Many parents seek illumination about the results of junior's IQ tests; is he a genius or an idiot? And then there was the lady with the ailing parakeet; it had diarrhea and she wanted to know what to do about it (unfortunately, our pamphlet on parakeets failed to supply the information, and we had to refer her to a pet shop).

Secretaries, either in person or by phone, are steady library users. And, as they work for all kinds of firms, they need all kinds of information—anything from statistics on census tracts to pictures of 1890 styles for an advertising campaign. And they ask about spelling—anything from simple everyday words to scientific ones ("The boss said he thought it was spelled this way, but I thought I'd better check with the library").

And students—more and more students—if the *1969 Statistical Abstract of the United States* is correct in its enrollment predictions.

	1968	1985
At the secondary level	14,145,000	17,345,000
At the college level	6,801,000	11,846,000

Although varying from area to area, from school to school and from semester to semester, students make up a considerable percentage of library users. And their requests cover every field of recorded knowledge. One moment you may be asked for debate material on lowering the voting age, the next for biographical material about an author.

Also varying, widely, is student knowledge of how to get at the material needed. Some students tackle the catalog and indexes with enthusiasm and efficiency, needing assistance only with reference materials or specialized tools. Others wander aimlessly, like the proverbial lost souls. Librarians soon learn to keep an eye out for the latter, students who must be rescued and taught the basic how-to-do-it techniques.

Call it teaching or call it helping, in a public library dispensing information on how to find something is an all-important part of the adult librarian's work, not only with students but with the general public.

If you work in the main library of a large system, you will be a reference librarian in a department—a specialist, in other words. With its extensive collection of book and nonbook materials (magazines, pamphlets and documents, microfilms), the main library functions as the city or county information center. As such, it serves individuals and organizations of all kinds, and operates as the backup for the network of community branches.

If, on the other hand, you work in a branch or a medium-size independent library, you will also be answering questions. You will be expected to ferret out information, in less detail, on many subjects—anything from addresses of congressmen to who invented the zero. In other words, you will be a generalist. Also, you will usually be involved with selecting the collection, deciding what materials will best serve your particular community. And, because you have a closer relationship with your public, you will often act as a reader's adviser.

Sometimes the advice sought is not merely for library materials. Take the case of the middle-aged woman who announced that her children were now grown and she "needed a purpose in life." Would the library please

suggest one? Or the young couple who spent several days
investigating the draft laws, then asked for information
about Canada and, finally, wanted advice on whether or
not to take that drastic step. In neither case, of course,
could the library provide the solution, only information
on which decisions could be reached. But talking to an
interested and sympathetic librarian may have helped.

The developing cooperative systems offer challenging
opportunities for the adult reference librarian. At the
large reference center you might be a subject specialist
from a department, or you might be a generalist working with all departments; some networks are using one
approach, some the other. In a medium-size library, an
in-between link in the system, you would be a generalist.

Some of the requests reaching the reference centers require persistent detective work, often requiring outside
contacts. Take the case of alligators in the New York
sewer system, for instance. A patron in the San Francisco
area had heard that people who had bought them as
babies, for pets, got scared when they began to grow and
flushed them down the toilets.

The only allusion the reference staff could find in the
library was in Thomas Pychon's novel *V*. In it one of the
characters joins a patrol assigned to New York City's
sewers to kill alligators which had grown enormous, and
had become blind and albino from dwelling in darkness.

At a dead end, San Francisco queried the appropriate
department in New York. According to the Commissioner of the Environmental Protection Administration,
they have had inquiries from all over the world on this
subject. His reply may have disappointed the patron:
"I know of no verified instance of survival of alligators

in our system. As you suggested, the alligators that are found are of the pet variety that exit from households through a convenient flush tank. It is likely that the alligators grow from nine inches to nine feet (a size I have heard mentioned) in the repeated telling of the story rather than in our sewers."

Whether you are a specialist or a generalist, you have behind-the-scenes duties. You may be responsible for the picture or pamphlet collection, for a quick reference file on many subjects or for a specialized-information file (literary criticism, for example). You may be in charge of processing new books, of inventory or of replacing materials worn out or lost. These are some of the many tasks, invisible to the public, which must be dealt with if a library is to adequately serve that public.

Role of the Children's Librarian

In 1803 a Boston bookseller, Caleb Bingham by name, donated 150 books to his hometown of Salisbury, Conn. These volumes, considered suitable for young people between the ages of nine and 16, established the first library for children.

To be sure, as far back as the time of Benjamin Franklin, there had been apprentice libraries, used by young men eager to advance their education. The young men were very young, for until child-labor laws came into existence boys could be apprenticed at 12 years of age. One such library even permitted girls to use it—once a week, for one whole hour.

There were also Sunday School libraries. Although their religious tracts and books reflected the views of a particular sect, and usually harped upon sin and salvation, the children could read them at home without paying a penny.

During the early decades of the 19th century the demand for education for the many, to meet the needs of an increasingly industrialized society, gained momentum. In 1852 Massachusetts passed the first compulsory school attendance law. Gradually, as more children learned to read, it became apparent that special collections for young readers would be necessary. It was the public library, rather than the school system, that shouldered the responsibility of meeting this new community need.

In the beginning, the children's books were often tucked away in corridors or alcoves. But, as more and more children visited the libraries, separate quarters were set aside for them. During the last decade of the 19th century children's rooms opened across the country, from Massachusetts to Colorado. In 1906 Anne Carroll Moore, one of the pioneers in work with young people, opened the Children's Department of the New York Public Library. With the groundwork laid, by the time the Carnegie building program got under way, space was provided for the use of young people.

During this period adult attitudes toward children underwent slow, but striking, changes. Until then children had been regarded as almost nonpersons, victims of the stern Puritan to-be-seen-and-not-heard point of view. For the most part, they were thought of as miniature adults—charming creatures prone to troublesome tantrums who one day become men and women.

A changing viewpoint mirrored an awakening interest in children for their own sakes. A child began to be thought of as an individual, and childhood as a time of life with its own rights—the right to imagine and learn on its own level, the right to read not only for instruction but for sheer pleasure, the right to a literature of its own.

Alice began her adventures in 1865, *Little Women* appeared in 1868 and *Kim* in 1899, to name but a few. Books began to be written specifically for boys and girls, and publishers began to establish separate juvenile departments. In 1919 Children's Book Week was inaugurated. The John Newbery Medal, for the most distinguished children's book of the year, was first awarded in 1922; several years later, in 1938, the Caldecott Medal was presented for the best illustrated volume.

Over the years the number of titles published increased steadily. By 1950 there were 1,059 new books for young people; in 1960, 1,725; in 1965, 2,473 new books and 422 new editions of old ones.

Inevitably, such a tremendous output included much that was worthless if not outright bad, as well as much that was well written and imaginatively illustrated. To evaluate the growing literature the *Horn Book* began publication in 1924. Devoted to children's books and to juvenile authors and illustrators, this outstanding magazine still serves librarians, teachers and interested parents. in addition, publication such as the *Saturday Review* and *The New York Times Book Review* evaluate children's books on a regular basis. Children's literature has, of necessity, developed its own standards of criticism.

Over the years, children's literature, also of necessity, has developed its own librarians. The first to establish courses for children's librarians, in 1899, was the Pratt Institute's School of Library Training. The following year the Carnegie Library of Pittsburgh organized its own training program. From then on, as library schools were established, juvenile literature and work with young people were part of the curriculum. And many libraries worked out on-the-job training programs. Today a children's department is an accepted part of any organization chart; specialized courses for training children's librarians are part of any library school curriculum.

Specialist or Generalist?

As a matter of fact, a children's librarian is both a specialist and a generalist. With her thorough knowledge of juvenile literature she functions as a specialist. It is she who selects which materials will be in the collection. Procedures vary from library to library, but one way or another the children's librarian looks at new books and decides which ones to order. In addition, there are evaluation meetings to discuss books already in the collection, what to keep and what to discard.

It also helps to have a flair for acting. For she gives book talks and conducts story hours in the library, and usually visits nearby classrooms. The close cooperation with the schools which launched childrens' programs in the 19th century has continued in the 20th, as many elementary schools do not yet have their own libraries.

In all these respects the children's librarian is a specialist. But in other respects she is a generalist. She must know a little bit about an enormous range of subjects, for she is asked for material about everything, from astronauts to zebras. Furthermore, in all except the largest libraries, she has to know the basic adult reference tools, for in nearly all other libraries she will be *the* librarian on night duty at least once a week, and will be working with adults and young adults.

Besides being both a specialist and a generalist, the children's librarian is a library's strongest link with the community, for the children's room serves as a center of information and guidance for adults concerned with young people—parents and teachers and, increasingly, social workers. If she can think and talk on her feet, she will be in demand as a speaker at PTA meetings and other community functions.

Finally, the children's librarian plans special projects. During one Children's Book Week in Hollywood, Calif., for example, more than a hundred enthralled youngsters watched a magician—the magician in question being a poised 12-year-old performer. Another branch in the area held an author's party.

Not every community, however, has such resources at its disposal—especially not in the disadvantaged areas, where imagination and ingenuity are often a librarian's main assets.

The Hobby Club in one such library collected plain ordinary bottles of all shapes and sizes. When they are covered with colorful tissue paper and shellacked, there is a stained glass effect. Coffee cans, similarly treated, were turned into canisters and made a nice gift for Mom. This particular project concentrated on things that could be done and used at home.

Another Hobby Club stressed the use of books. Paper bags became masks with designs adapted from books on African art. Using Federal funds for paper and printing, one area inaugurated the "chain game." With each book the children received a gaily colored slip for written comments which might later appear on bookmarks.

In cooperation with the local school one library launched the Bookbaggers. This project had a specific objective, to help poor readers, and the librarian worked closely with the remedial teacher. To spark the children's interest, films and games as well as storytelling were put to use. Augmenting the activities in the school and the library were block visits, aimed at including the adult community.

These are only a few experiments, in one city. Such examples can be multiplied by the hundreds as public libraries across the country are devising new ways of reaching out into their communities.

Planning Ahead

If you want to specialize in service to children, there are several subjects about which you will need to know something:

1. child psychology
2. current social issues
3. methods for teaching reading
4. subject matter of the school curriculum
5. audiovisual materials and techniques

Not that you need be an expert in any of these fields, but you will need some basic information about all of them. So keep these subjects in mind when mapping out your undergraduate program.

Adult and children's services, growing and changing for over a century, constitute a long-established pattern. More recently, two new services—young adult and audiovisual—have evolved.

The New Age Group: Young Adult Service

During the 1920s, work with adolescents was limited to 14-to-16-year-olds whose family finances forced them to leave school. These early collections emphasized vocational training and continuing-education materials, how-to-do-it books, the classics and some popular fiction. Later, as the United States reluctantly relinquished its isolationism, books about other countries were added. But otherwise, until World War II, the scope of such collections changed little.

Before the war ended, many a teen-ager had joined the labor force. With money in his pocket and a broader outlook, he was certainly no longer a child—nor was he yet an adult. The noted anthropologist Margaret Mead has pointed out that young people in the United States resemble a separate tribe with its own rules and taboos, with its own interests and objectives—a kind of subculture.

After the war the development of separate library departments for the 13-19 age group reflected this emerging social pattern. In the publishing world it was the period of the junior novel. Almost without exception, these stories emphasized middle-class, middle-income life and values. Their high school heroes and heroines were concerned with dating and popularity, with sports and success.

J. D. Salinger's *Catcher in the Rye* was published in 1951. First college and soon high school students adopted it as "their" book. With its down-to-earth language and a hero at odds with himself, his family and society, it created a storm of controversy. As the heated debate raged, one thing became clear—many young people wanted books that tackled real problems, not tinsel tales that ignored or skirted them.

Then came 1957 and the curriculum changes generated by Sputnik. In pursuit of information for class reports or term papers, students invaded the libraries. This frenzied search for knowledge brought into sharp focus the still unanswered, often debated question: was the young adult collection for recreational reading only, or should it also provide supplementary material for school assignments? At the height of the Sputnik panic the students provided an interim answer; they had no time for recreational reading. And today, as you know, the college-bound student can find few hours for purely pastime reading.

For years the pros and cons of this topic were debated—with inconclusive results—at library conventions and in the professional journals. Some libraries adopted one approach, some the other. Meanwhile, the young adults answered the question for themselves. They used the library for assignments and, while they were there, picked up a book on chess or surfing or Gibran's *The Prophet*. Leisure time, if any, was spent on records and transistor radios, TV and movies tailored for the young audience. They could afford them, the young adults from middle-class families, part of the affluent society.

And those other young adults, off in a ghetto or run-down neighborhood—what did they want and need? The question was academic. Only a tiny percentage ever used the library.

When the sores of American society opened up in the mid-1960s, the question ceased to be academic. It was all too easily answered. Librarians discovered that young adults in the disadvantaged areas desperately needed both recreation and information. They also discovered that in this nation, with its high literacy rate, many young adults did not read easily, that some were functionally illiterate. So, perforce, audiovisual materials and imagination have been the most valuable tools in the impoverished communities.

We have already seen what one inventive young adult librarian did in a potentially explosive situation. A group of five libraries south of San Francisco has tackled quite a different condition. The librarians go out into the communities to locate the young adults, to find out what kind of service might lure them into a librarylike situation and to make them aware of what the library can do for them.

The project experiments with any and all means of communication. For books, nearly all paperbacks, there are "satellites"—spinner-style racks in places frequented by young adults: recreation centers, parks, youth and Economic Opportunity centers. Posters and hand tools—yes, hand tools—may be checked out. A few typewriters are available for overnight use. And, of course, records and films.

There are many programs, the only set one being a weekly film showing. Most of the get-togethers are impromptu—group discussions, one-to-one talk sessions, sing-alongs and guitar playing, jam and carpentry sessions. Mostly, however, there is talk—with the adults listening. (Listening, participating adults have found out, is a good way to close the generation gap.)

This project has been an example of how the library has really reached out. Virtually all federally funded young-adult projects have, in essence, been programs of reaching out to bring in. There have been successes, and there have been failures; there has been frustration, and there has been exhilaration. But one thing has been firmly established by these demonstration programs— the policy of reaching out to involve young adults. You, the new librarians, will provide the momentum to keep this policy going.

Now and New

In a speech at the 1969 American Library Association convention, author Nat Hentoff commented that the goal of education, including what goes on in libraries, should be to create "men who will remake themselves and then go on to remake society."

It was quite a convention. A group of young librarians arose in wrath to demand that the library world remake itself to keep up with the times, so that it can help to remake our ailing society.

And listen to what some high school panelists had to say:

". . . The young person today is completely different from the older person, who wants things to stay as they are, whereas the young person wants to learn and learn for the purpose of changing things."

"The library has an extra responsibility. . . . This world has many problems, and the responsibility of the library is to get the proper books, the proper films and other programs to help the student and the young person learn about these problems and come to some conclusion about them. . . ."

"The major emphasis in this discussion has been on books. . . . This is not a world of books. . . . It's a world of other media, other ways of communication and ways of learning things. . . . If the library is to become successful, it is going to have to use these other methods. . . ."

". . . The type of personnel that works in the library is also very important. . . . I'm not talking about things like whether a librarian is young or old. . . . I think it's more important that you have people who are interested in helping the students rather than there to collect a salary or yell at the kids to be quiet."

That's what is new. That's what is happening now.

Today every library, large or small, can serve the young adults in its community. Tomorrow? Listen to Nat Hentoff again.

The library is going to be the center for independent inquiry, and they're going to be coming to you not only to find out what you know but who you are. . . .

That's what all young people are about now, finding a life that has meaning, and you can either help them or get out of their way.

Whether you become a young-adult librarian concerned mainly with the 13-19 age group or whether teenagers are merely one part of your responsibility, you can make the library come alive for them. You can help them learn and think, not only because knowledge is necessary for a job or to pass the college entrance examination but because learning is a pleasure. You can help them enjoy and evaluate. You can help them "find a life that has meaning."

In the years ahead, working with young adults will be important as never before. As far as libraries are concerned, they *are* the population explosion. In 1965 the 15-19 age group in the United States numbered 17,051,000; the estimate for 1975 is 20,879,000.

What the Young-Adult Librarian Does

Selects and maintains the collection of printed materials.
As this is a fluid collection, you must keep up with ever-changing interests.

Plans special programs and exhibits.
As these usually involve films, records, posters, etc., you will need an interest in and some knowledge of audiovisual materials.

Helps students with library tools; how to use the catalog, indexes, etc. All librarians do this, but it is a special responsibility of the young-adult librarian. So it will be a great asset if you like to teach.

Training Needed

Master's degree (see Chapter X)

Basic knowledge of certain nonlibrary fields.
Survey courses in education and sociology.
Adolescent psychology, with particular attention to the needs of the young adult in our society.

Audiovisual materials and their effective use. (As the fifth year of graduate study allows little opportunity for nonlibrary courses, plan to work these subjects into your undergraduate program.)

The Young Adult Librarian Should Be:

Creative and imaginative. Flexible and "unshockable."
Gay and outgoing. Intellectually curious. Socially con-

scious. People-oriented, with a *genuine* affinity for young people.

A tall order. But the young adult of today will ignore the librarian who lacks these qualities and qualifications.

V

THE PUBLIC LIBRARY
CITY AND COUNTY
Audiovisual—Bookmobiles—Behind-the-Scenes

The New Media: The Audiovisual Department

In 1877 Edison produced the first cylinder; in 1889 he collaborated with other inventors to produce the first motion picture. In 1914 the library in St. Paul, Minn., established a record collection; in 1929 the library in Kalamazoo, Mich., began to circulate films.

During the next decade here and there across the country libraries experimented with ways of handling nonprint materials. For the most part, such materials were treated as embarrassing relatives who must be housed and maintained, but ignored as much as possible. Or they were regarded as fads that, it was hoped, would fade away. Especially where Hollywood films were concerned, the library world tended to think of them as merely extensions of the books on which they were based.

The number of films produced, and the uses to which they were put, increased steadily during World War II. Film as a method of day-to-day communication was here to stay. Recognizing this fact, in 1947 the Carnegie Corporation financed a study of how the public library could use films to further its objectives in the community. At about the same time, the American Library Association established a Film Advisory Service.

The 1950s were, in the main, years of reorganization, with many libraries consolidating separate record and film collections. The 1960s were years of steady, if not spectacular, growth. When one large system first opened an audiovisual service, it offered its patrons 90 films and less than 200 records; by 1968 it had acquired 1,000 16-mm. sound films and 15,000 recordings.

Today most audiovisual departments include:

1. *Motion pictures* of the documentary or informational type, covering a wide range of subjects—art and music, people and places, history and government, medicine and health, sports and adventure, literature, perhaps personnel training. Films are usually available for outside use, but many libraries cannot provide projectors.

2. *Recordings,* both musical and nonmusical. Originally, most musical collections consisted of serious music representing the world's great composers and artists. Many now include popular recordings by outstanding performers or records illustrative of emerging musical forms. The nonmusical collection includes dramatic and literary selections by actors or authors, the recorded voices of historical figures, United Nations proceedings, foreign-language courses. In some libraries records may be taken out; in others they must be used on the premises.

3. *Microrecorded materials*—microfilms, microcards

and microprint, issues of newspapers and magazines, census and genealogical records, United Nations documents. As the techniques of miniaturization develop there will doubtless be additions to these collections—microfiche, for example.

4. *Picture collections.* Over the years libraries have developed picture files, some of them very large and extremely valuable for artists, researchers, etc. In some cases they have been brought together with other visual materials; in others they have remained a separate unit.

5. *Other materials.* Filmstrips and slides. There are large and excellent collections in schools and colleges, but not in great demand in public libraries. Tape recordings and videotapes. These are of increasing interest but not yet generally available in public libraries.

As the racks of records and reels of film accumulated, so did indexes and directories, until today the audiovisual librarian has at his disposal tools similar to those used by book librarians. Over the years many departments have developed their own indexes for films and records, for pictures and micromaterials. And there is a growing literature of directories and guides—the *Wilson Educational Film Guide,* the *Educator's Guide to Free Films,* a special *Guide for Religious Films* and one for *Children's Record Reviews, U.S. Government Films for Public Use* and the *Library of Congress Film Catalog.*

In addition, the audiovisual librarian is frequently a program planner, for many patrons who consult this department need not only a certain film but a program. To serve such a patron well requires time and tact, a highly specialized knowledge of film content and sources, as well as technical expertize and an ability to work with groups. In other words, the librarian functions as a specialist in his field, as does the reference librarian in the literature or business department.

By the mid-1960s, then, the audiovisual department was a going and growing operation in many libraries. But it was often a department beset by many problems, some of them apparently insoluble.

Some of the obstacles were practical. Except for the very new buildings, libraries had not been constructed with audiovisual materials or equipment in mind. In large buildings this meant squeezing the newest department into some little-used space and remodeling it—an expensive procedure. In most cases small libraries found it difficult to make use of audiovisual materials because, with no separate room available, the showing of a film disturbed patrons who wanted to study or browse in peace.

And there was the continuous battle of the budget. Library funds are rarely adequate, let alone ample. And films especially are expensive, much more expensive than books. Print-oriented librarians have been loath to see money drained away from already inadequate book budgets. The same held true for equipment; if audiovisual got a new projector, some other department might have to do without a much-needed pamphlet file.

The result was an either-or polarization that reflected the principal difficulty, a philosophical one. Most librarians were firmly, some stubbornly, print-oriented. Most were not greatly interested in, some were openly hostile to, nonprint materials. Most thought of the audiovisual department as a sort of annex, physical and philosophical, to the "real" library. Consequently, audiovisual librarians not only usually had to fight for every dollar, but were often unable to make maximum use of their materials.

Then, in the mid-1960s, came a breakthrough. Spawned by violence (riots) and by impending disaster (seething urban unrest), various Federal projects were launched. Suddenly, audiovisual departments had the two things they most needed—money and freedom, freedom to experiment.

The main purpose of these projects in disadvantaged areas was to reach nonreaders, many of them undereducated, who would never think of a library as an "in" place. What was needed was attention-getting material for people who were not print-oriented. What was also needed was an imaginative, energetic staff. Federal funds provided both, and libraries began to jump.

The Countee Cullen Library in Harlem is an example of what can be accomplished with money and imagination. This branch, named after the well-known poet who had taught in a nearby school, had once been a neighborhood cultural center. But because of staff shortages and a limited collection (i.e., not enough money), the better-educated and regularly employed readers were using branches closer to their jobs. To those with less education and only occasional employment the library had little or no appeal.

In addition to an enlarged staff, Federal funds provided the equipment essential for the use of nonprint materials—blackout shades so that films could be shown during the day, projectors and screens, films and filmstrips, records and tape recordings. The rooms were made more attractive, the procedures more informal.

Jazz concerts, poetry and dramatic readings, health programs—all attracted large audiences. Figures tell the story. The year before the project was launched, 6,000 people visited the branch for group activities; the first year of the project, 16,000; the second year, 30,000.

Across the country the program varied according to the needs and resources of the particular community. For example, the Venice branch near Los Angeles used Federal funds to rent full-length films for special occasions: *Viva Zapata* for a Mexican-American celebration of Cinco de Mayo, a celebration for which the library also mounted a full-fledged fiesta; *Raisin in the Sun* for the black community; and *Invaders From Mars,* an old Buster Crabbe film, for science fiction addicts.

They tapped any and all sources for high-interest films. Consulates and tourist bureaus, for example, donated films around which programs were built.

All of the federally funded projects made an all-out effort to attract young adults. And they proved that carefully thought-out, well-executed programs using audiovisual materials will bring this age group to the library. This has proved true not only in the disadvantaged areas but in the affluent ones as well.

This unarguable fact may well decide the future, not only of the audiovisual service but of the public library itself. As one member of the Venice staff put it: "If we are not prepared to meet the demands of the young people, they are going to destroy public libraries by refusing to vote for bond issues when they are of voting age. Their fathers and mothers have already defeated bond issues. As a young girl said to me recently: 'I guess we are going to have a separate library system for films and records if the library can't do the job.'"

Is the public library going to be able to do the job? There is no pat answer to that difficult question. But there are indications that the audiovisual service is beginning to be regarded as an important and integral part of library functions.

In 1968 there appeared a new version of *Guidelines and Standards for Public Library Service*. It recommended that an area, or regional, library have a film collection of at least 1,000 film title, as well as sufficient duplicate copies of popular films to meet borrower demand. At least 50 new titles should be added each year, and the library should have the necessary equipment and staff for inspection and cleaning of the films. In addition, this type of library should provide a collection of 50 films for each of the smaller community branches in its area. As to recording, there should be at least 10,000 albums, with 3,000 new recordings added annually.

The large research library should have at least 4,000 16-mm.-film titles, as well as slides, filmstrips, videotapes and other audiovisual materials. This is to include a reference collection of historic and current subjects and should consist of at least 50,000 albums.

To be sure, these are guidelines, recommendations for standards hopefully to be achieved. But the significance of these nonprint guidelines is far-reaching. What is being suggested is that collections should provide materials in whatever form they happen to exist.

What is this going to mean to you, the library user? When you are looking for material about modern American poets, the librarian should not only tell you about books and magazines, but point out that there are records of Robert Frost and Carl Sandburg reading their own poetry. When you are doing a term paper on some aspect of the United Nations, you should be told about the material on microfilm. When a bibliography about space is compiled, it should include not only books and pamphlets, but recordings and films as well.

As the 1970s begin, audiovisual service is at a crossroads. One way leads to integration of print and nonprint materials. The other continues along on its separate path. Which road it will take is unclear, and the route may vary from library to library.

But one thing is clear. One way or another, the demand for nonprint materials will have to be met. The problems of getting audiovisual materials to the public must be solved. And in the decade ahead new librarians will be seeking the solution.

Bookmobiles

"Bookmobile" means, literally, books in motion. Today you may encounter books in motion along lonely rutted back roads or poking through the cluttered streets of a city ghetto.

The first bookmobile was really a book wagon. Back in 1905 the imaginative librarian of Hagerstown, Md., with the help of an adventurous janitor, began service to nearby farming areas. Doubling as driver, the janitor took charge of the converted wagon, equipped to carry 250 books. The wagon was a cross between a grocer's delivery wagon and a hearse, and some of the farming people called it "the dead wagon." But business was very much alive at the 30 stations at which the book wagon stopped. The janitor drove the team of horses along byways, winding through 500 square miles, over 16 routes, and taking four days for the round trip.

In 1910 the book wagon came to an untimely end when it was hit by a freight train. Neither the pioneering janitor-driver nor the horses were hurt, but the wagon was a total wreck. The following year a public-spirited citizen donated $2,500 for a new bookmobile. Dobbin, however, was replaced by an automobile, a car with a specially equipped chassis.

Somewhat later another itinerant library began taking books to some 20 mining villages and camps in Minnesota. Since the miners had emigrated from many lands, its collection included books in many languages: Finnish, Norwegian and Swedish, French and German, Spanish and Portuguese, Slovenian, Serbian, Russian and Polish.

By 1920 Portland, Ore., had put the first bookmobile in the West on the road. And in 1936 the Ventura County Library began bookmobile service in California. During the Depression, bookmobile activity remained stagnant or was cut back. But limited though it was, records show that books from vans helped families through those gruelling years. There was one man, for instance, who kept his family clothed and fed by raising rabbits, using the information he found on a roving bookmobile.

After World War II, bookmobile service increased dramatically. In 1937 there were only 60 bookmobiles in the entire United States; by 1950 there were more than 600 and by 1956, more than 900. In that year came the Library Services Act, followed by the more extensive Library Services and Construction Act. One of the original provisions called for an extension of library service to areas with populations of 10,000 or less. Result: 375 more bookmobiles rolled along the highways and bounced over country roads.

In areas never before served, regular stops were established. New Mexico alone added over a hundred outlets in the rugged northern mountain territory, with its many Spanish-speaking and Indian villages. Arizona had never provided money for an extension service until the legislature appropriated funds to match those available from the Federal Government. As one enthusiastic bookmobile patron commented: "This is the best thing that has happened to us since they paved the roads."

By 1963 there were 1,400 bookmobiles in the United States. There were nearly 2,000 in 1965, even before the impact of the Library Services and Construction Act had begun to be felt. This statute provided Federal grants to states for the purpose of extending public library service to areas without any or with inadequate facilities. That is, it broadened the scope of the programs to include urban as well as rural communities. It added construction of new buildings and expansion of existing ones, and included books and equipment for new libraries. And these new "buildings" have numbered among them the many bookmobiles now roaming the streets of Watts, Brooklyn, Cleveland, Atlanta—virtually every major city in the country.

Bookmobiles also provide a link between the outside world and certain isolated segments of society. They visit hospitals and schools for the handicapped, go behind the walls of prisons and correctional institutions and crawl up mountain roads to ranger stations. They are beginning to stop at retirement centers, in both rural and urban areas. Because of physical disabilities or lack of transportation, many people living in such communities cannot get to libraries, so there is a growing movement to bring libraries to them.

One place the public library will visit less is the school.

In the past, many schools, especially at the elementary level, relied on the public library to bring nontextbook material to them. Recently, however, Federal funds have helped to establish libraries in schools which had none and to improve inadequate collections.

Books are carried not only on wheels. Even in the early days books were circulated from canal boats in Washington, D.C. In the mountains of Kentucky and Tennessee there were four-legged bookmobiles as mules carried fodder for the mind as well as for the body. Streetcars have been used in Europe, and today one Swedish library runs book trains through the countryside on Sundays. Jeeps are used in Puerto Rico, and airplanes in remote areas of Alaska and the American Southwest.

Originally, a standard bookmobile served an isolated Indian reservation in New Mexico. The 200-mile round trip over bad dirt roads was hazardous even in good weather. Snow or rain made it impossible, and it had to be discontinued. But the reservation still gets books. Nowadays the manager of the nearby trading post flies his plane to the largest town in the area, where he is met by the Northwestern Regional Library Bookmobile. Acting as the librarian, he selects materials for about 50 families, exchanging them every three months. The idea was the manager's, and it has been incorporated as part of the regular service.

Since so much of the earth's surface is water, boatmobiles have been a natural development. For years Norway and Sweden have transported books by bus. But much of the area's rugged coastline has no roads, so boatmobiles were launched to reach remote coastal towns. Mexico, too, has boatmobiles, as do some of our inland waterways of

Atlantic Coast states. In Thailand, a country of canals, the U.S. Information Service obtained a boat to carry materials upcountry. And throughout the world UNESCO has been bringing books to people, adopting whatever means of transportation suits the terrain. Today, all over the world, books are in motion.

And not only books, for a bus or a boat can also haul projectors and phonographs, films and records. Increasingly, bookmobiles are stocking nonprint materials, and the librarian aboard needs to be skilled in the audiovisual field.

The bookmobile librarian needs to be physically strong. It is a hectic existence, with the crowds that throng into and around the van, with a tight schedule of several stops a day. He must be an enthusiastic salesman. With only limited samples, he must convince people of all ages of the value and pleasure to be derived from his wares.

Above all, the bookmobile librarian must be friendly and people-oriented. He comes to know his patrons as individuals, not merely as readers. Often he comes to know them socially, being invited into their homes or sharing a freshly baked pie at the van. In the rural areas, many a librarian has run errands in town for his patrons, carried messages or helped out in an emergency. In the city, he has helped to solve many a family problem, explaining how to fill out job applications or which government agency to contact for some desperately needed assistance.

Life on a bookmobile can be an exciting adventure. But it is not for the timid or the scholarly introvert, or for those who prefer a leisurely pace.

Helping People to Help Themselves. Work with the disadvantaged.

Who, exactly, are the disadvantaged?

In a 1964 issue of the *Library Journal* an adult educator pinpointed five groups of the disadvantaged which could be helped by the public library. Five years later the same groups still desperately need all the help they can get, and that need is all too likely to continue for years to come.

The five groups:

1. The young—particularly the school dropouts under 21.
2. The old—people over 65.
3. The people who are functionally illiterate and may be anywhere along the age spectrum.
4. The "new immigrants" from rural areas and small towns—people displaced by the mechanization of agriculture and flocking to the cities because there is literally no other place for them to go.
5. The Negroes, who make up the majority of each of the other four groups.

What will the librarian working with the disadvantaged be doing? To this question there is no neat, predictable answer, for life is neither neat nor predictable in a city ghetto or barrio or on an Indian reservation.

He may be on a bookmobile, playing records for children to dance to. He may be holding a read-in or showing movies. He may be preparing to publish a collection of stories by children or book reviews by teen-agers. All of this in addition to more traditional library activities.

The librarian who works with the disadvantaged needs to be part pioneer, part social worker, part psychologist. He needs to have not only the necessary professional knowledge but feeling as well. He must bring hope to areas where before there was only hopelessness. And this librarian needs a sense of adventure for he will be where the action is.

Behind the Scenes: Technical Services

Most public librarians deal directly with people. But not all of them. Without these invisible librarians no library could open its doors. No books or pamphlets, no films or records would ever reach the library. And no one would be able to find anything.

The Order Department

Procedures for ordering materials vary from library to library, but whatever the system used, once the choice is made someone has to order the physical items.

Take Los Angeles Public Library as an example. The order sheet of adult books which branches might want for their collections may be from 20 to 40 legal-size pages. Each of the more than 60 branches places an order. Add to these the orders for many books not included on the sheets that the departments at the main library need. Further add the separate order sheets for children's books. Obviously, the order department of a big city or county library is a complicated operation requiring a large staff.

Many nonbook materials, other than pamphlets, must be ordered and checked in. This is usually handled by a serials division, which may be a separate unit or be part of the order department. And what are serials? Among other things they include newspapers and magazines, publications of learned societies, annual publications (almanacs, etc.), all government documents (Federal and state, city and county, foreign and United Nations). That article in a particular magazine, that U.N. report you needed for your term paper—someone had to order them.

Order departments have been in danger of being buried by an avalanche of order sheets and card files. Serials divisions have been in danger of being buried by fallout from the information explosion. But fortunately this phase of library operations is one most easily rescued by the computer, most adaptable to data processing.

In San Francisco, for example, the library has print-outs of its magazines, newspapers and selected serials. These several catalogs provide the user with information in alphabetical listing, by title and subject. The computer provides a considerable amount of helpful, time-saving information, such as cross-references. It might inform you that the *American Economic Association Papers and Proceedings* is indexed in the index to the *American Economic Review,* that the title varies or that it was formerly known as such and such; if its back files are on microfilm, you will be apprised of this fact. It also provides a daily list for each department, as well as weekly and monthly cumulative reports. Once a month the computer searches its records and tells the library what periodicals should be going to the bindery.

This is one system already in use. And today many large libraries are beginning to employ computers and data processing to gain control of the paper deluge created by the information explosion.

Catalog Department

When you are working on a term paper, sooner or later you will probably find yourself consulting a catalog. The majority of libraries still use card catalogs, but some have changed to computer print-out book catalogs. Without a catalog, whether in card or book form, trying to find information on a specific subject is like looking for the proverbial needle in the haystack.

The library user searching for specific information resembles a detective—a detective in need of clues. And who provides the clues? A cataloger, or possibly several catalogers. You may never see a cataloger, but without his help you would find it difficult—if not impossible—to find information about anything.

What does he do, this invisible person who is usually a subject specialist? To begin with, he examines a new book to determine its content. He then searches the master catalog to find out its relation to other books already in the collection. Next, using accepted catalog rules, he describes it; that is, he decides under whose name it will appear and what features or unique characteristics will identify it. In addition, he analyzes the contents more closely to determine the subject interest and subject heading.

In other words, the cataloger tells you, the user, what materials a library has by a given author, what titles it has, on what subjects information is available, what books it has on a given subject.

The cataloger has another, related task. He selects the

numbers, or combination of letters and numbers, which indicate the subject of the publication, and which place it on the shelves with other volumes on the same subject. In other words, the cataloger provides all the clues. Without him any library, large or small, would be an insoluble maze, a hopeless jumble. And you would never finish that term paper.

This is obviously a time-consuming and costly procedure, so many libraries use the catalog cards available from the Library of Congress. And another company specializing in library publications and services, the H. W. Wilson Company, also provides cards used primarily by small libraries.

Circulation Department

Today the circulation desk in many libraries is manned by clerks or clerk typists (see Chapter XI). The librarian is, again, usually invisible—except when summoned to soothe an irate patron waving an overdue notice and protesting that he knows for a fact that he did return that particular item.

The librarian may be invisible, but he is very busy, formulating policies and procedures for the many transactions that take place across the circulation desk—transactions which include registering users and issuing and receiving materials.

At the present time, especially, the circulation librarian's position is a policy-making one. Circulation problems and procedures are well suited to automation, using data-processing systems to record the return of materials and send overdue notices. Those print-outs the clerk may check before issuing you a card show if you are in good standing with the computer.

Many libraries have, or are already in the process of adapting, some version of automative techniques to their needs. And it is the circulation librarian who must work closely with the automation expert to develop procedures most applicable to the particular library or library system.

Bindery Department

Have you ever wanted to find a book you had previously used? You are not certain of either the author or the title, but it is about exploration of space and you are sure that you will recognize it when you see it. It was a red book. But none of the books in that section fit the image you have in mind, and for a very good reason. Since you used it, perhaps a year ago, it had to be rebound. It has been to the bindery and has returned—a blue book.

Bindery is big business. In a recent year The Los Angeles Public Library sent 125,690 volumes to a commercial bindery and repaired more than 89,000 in the department; in addition, some 17,000 pamphlets and 3,500 musical scores were bound.

Book repairers do mend and repair books, but they also do a lot of other things. They affix plastic covers to many new books, reinforce magazine covers and maps and put the lettering on the spines of various types of materials.

Usually it is a librarian who coordinates the many operations of a bindery department and supervises a large nonprofessional staff.

A librarian in any of these departments may have little or no direct contact with the public. But his objective is the same as that of the desk librarian—to serve that public. Without these departments a library would receive no materials, its patrons could not find anything in usable condition and nothing could be checked out or returned. They may be invisible, these departments and their librarians, but without them there would be no libraries.

FOR MORE INFORMATION

Brown, Eleanor. Bookmobiles and Bookmobile Service. Metuchen, N.J.: Scarecrow Press, 1967.

Conant, Ralph W., ed. *The Public Library and the City.* Cambridge, Mass.: Massachusetts Institute of Technology Press, 1965.

Role of the public library in a changing urban scene. New problems, new thinking, new concepts of service.

Coplan, Kate, and Castagna, Edwin. *The Library Reaches Out.* Dobbs Ferry, N.Y.: Oceana Publications, 1965.

Covers a wide range of library activities (including state and school libraries). Practical information on how to best serve a community.

Crosby, Harry H., and Bond, George R. *The McLuhan Explosion.* New York, N.Y.: American Book Company, 1968.

Gross, Elizabeth H. *Public Library Service to Children.* Dobbs Ferry, N.Y.: Oceana Publications, 1967.

Kujoth, Jean Spealman. *Readings in Non-Book Librarianship.* Metuchen, N.J.: Scarecrow Press, 1968.

Library Trends, October, 1968.

Issue devoted to young-adult service in the public library.

National Advisory Commission on Libraries. "Library Services for the Nation's Needs," *A.L.A. Bulletin,* October, 1968.

Peltier, E. J. "Toward Total Media Librarianship," *Film Library Quarterly,* Spring, 1968.

Top of the News.

A quarterly magazine published by the Children's Services Division and the Young Adult Services Division of the American Library Association.

Wilson Library Bulletin, November, 1969.

Includes several articles on audiovisual materials in public and school libraries.

VI

THE PUBLIC LIBRARY
FEDERAL AND STATE

FEDERAL LIBRARIES

You may not think of Federal or state libraries as "public" institutions; but they are tax-supported and therefore owned by the public. In 1876 the Librarian of Congress commented: "As the library of the American people, supported and constantly enlarged by taxation, it is eminently fitting that this library should not only be freely accessible to the whole people, but that it should furnish the fullest possible stores of information in every department of human knowledge."

Today thousands of libraries, within the United States and in many parts of the world, are owned and operated by the Federal Government. No other organization serves so many people. In its hospital libraries the Federal Government serves patients and supports medical research. It brings public library service to servicemen and their families in far corners of the globe. Its technical and specialized libraries provide legislators and policy-makers with the latest findings in their area, with balanced and accurate information on controversial subjects.

As a reference librarian in one of the larger libraries, you may be working on a long term project in the morning, on a rush request in the afternoon. In a smaller library, you may be running a one-man show. Or you may be working on improved techniques for handling the ever-growing flood of information.

Library of Congress

In April of 1800 Congress passed a law founding a library "for the purchase of such books as may be necessary for the use of Congress," and providing for housing them "in one suitable apartment."

By 1814 the Library of Congress consisted of more than 3,000 volumes, all of which were destroyed when the British set fire to the Capitol. The following year Congress authorized the purchase of Thomas Jefferson's private collection, consisting of some 6,000 books. One more fire, in 1851, plagued the national library when half of its 55,000 volumes went up in flames. Since that time, however, its growth has been both steady and spectacular until it is now the largest library in the United States, perhaps in the world. The 1967-68 annual report estimated the total collection to be 58,463,000.

Although the original nucleus consisted of books only, today its collection includes the records of man's achievements and failures, which have been brought together "from every region of the earth, from every age, by every means of transportation."

The many collections include:

Books and pamphlets, not only in English but in many languages.

Magazines of general interest and professional periodicals.

Newspapers, domestic and foreign.

Documents, Federal and state.

Maps, including early ones of the United States, and atlases of Ptolemy and Mercator.

Prints and photographs, notable among which is a Whistler collection and the Civil War photographs of Mathew B. Brady.

Slides, films and filmstrips, microfilm and microfiche.

Rare books—more than 2,000,000, ranging from medieval illuminated manuscripts to examples of current fine printing, and including the only perfect vellum copy of the Gutenberg Bible in the Western hemisphere.

Manuscripts—among them, Jefferson's rough draft of the Declaration of Independence; Washington's commission as commander in chief of the Continental Army; Lincoln's first and second drafts of the Gettysburg Address; papers of American statesmen and public leaders, from the time of Alexander Hamilton; papers of the presidents, from Washington to Coolidge (thereafter separate libraries have been established to collect and preserve Presidential papers).

Materials for the Blind—books in Braille and on magnetic tape, talking book records, as well as the necessary machines. Since 1931 the Division for the Blind has provided this service to blind residents of the United States and its possessions, and now distributes more than a million items a year.

Special subject collections include:

Music: sheet music and thousands of scores, holographs of master composers and American folk song.

Records: in addition to music, poetry and other readings, speeches.

Science: in 1866 the library acquired materials from the Smithsonian Institute and laid the foundation for its present outstanding collection.

Aeronautics: the largest in the world, it includes the papers of the Wright Brothers and the manuscript of Charles Lindbergh's *Spirit of St. Louis.*

Law: not only a complete collection of English and American publications, but an extensive collection of foreign law.

Orientalia: Chinese (the largest outside of China and Japan), Japanese and Korean, Turkish and Arabic, Tibetan, Manchurian and Mongolian.

Juvenile: a large collection of children's materials for the use of teachers and other adults (the library does not serve children).

To maintain its many collections and to render its many services, the library is organized into six departments, each having a number of divisions:

The Administrative Department is responsible for the maintenance and preservation of the collections and for the grounds and buildings—a considerable housekeeping chore when you consider that there are some 250 miles of bookshelves, 36 acres of floor space and 21 general and special reading rooms as well as study rooms. In addition, this department handles fiscal and protective services.

The Reference Department is in charge of both the general and specialized collections (except those of the Law Library). It has 17 divisions, including those for the blind and the handicapped. In a recent year it answered 975,000 requests for information (by phone or letter, or in person) and prepared 340 bibliographies.

The Law Library, primarily for the use of Congress, does legal research and provides necessary materials.

The Legislative Reference Service is the principal research and information center for Congress. In one year it answered more than 52,000 inquiries from individual members and committees. According to its statement of purpose: "It shall assist Members, committees and their staffs in analyzing, appraising, and evaluating pending and proposed legislation; it shall gather and analyze information on legislative issues and make this information available to the Congress without partisanship in selection or presentation." (Most of those papers you see the members shuffling at various hearings have come from this department.)

The Copyright Office registers claims for copyright protection and receives copies of books and other materials deposited with it.

The Processing Department involves various cataloging procedures, the card division, special services available to scholars and librarians.

Special services available include:

Printed catalog cards for books, and other materials, in its own collections and those sold to other libraries.

Bibliographies, guides and catalogs.

The *National Union Catalog* and the *Union List of Serials,* which provide researchers with valuable information as to the location of needed materials.

Cultural events sponsored by the library, ranging from concerts of chamber music to informational exhibits.

Experimental Projects

For more than 50 years the Library of Congress has conducted research, seeking better ways and means to organize and administer its many large, and ever-growing, collections. The results of this research in library technology have been made available to libraries throughout the country.

At present, as indicated in the discussion of technological change, the library is at work on the application of computer technology to library operations. In the future, as computer-based systems develop, the library will serve as a storehouse of information and a clearinghouse of experience. In the meantime, it will continue to initiate and develop experimental projects. And it will continue to serve Congress and the Federal agencies, scholars and researchers and the library world.

Opportunities in the Library of Congress

The Librarian of Congress, appointed by the President with the consent of the Senate, heads a staff of about 2,700, including hundreds of linguists and subject specialists. In other words, the stronger your specialized skills, the better your opportunity, although the generalist is by no means excluded. Also worth remembering is the fact that experience at the library will prove an invaluable asset for future assignments anywhere in the library world.

More information about the Library of Congress can be found in its annual reports (available at any large library). Also, inquiries on all matters of employment are welcomed. Write:

> Placement Officer
> Section 01
> Personnel Office
> Library of Congress
> Washington, D.C. 20540

National Archives

Actually, the full name is the National Archives and Records Service, and it consists of four operations.

"The National Archives," states an inscription on the outside of its building, "holds in trust the records of our national life and symbolizes our faith in the permanency of our national Institutions."

What the archives contain, in effect, is the basic information about the history and government of the United States from its beginning. On permanent display in the Exhibition Hall are the Declaration of Independence, the Constitution and the Bill of Rights. Stored in its stacks are the documents which have shaped our destiny—the Treaty of Paris, which ended the Revolution; Admiral Perry's reports on the opening of Japan; abolitionist petitions of Thoreau and Emerson; Lincoln's Emancipation Proclamation; the receipt for the purchase of Alaska; and the Japanese and German surrender documents ending World War II.

However, the archives is no musty warehouse. Every year it answers more than 400,000 questions—and some of the answers have changed the course of world history. When the Normandy invasion was being plotted, weather experts studied thousands of Weather Bureau reports going back many years in order to pinpoint the best date. When the Pentagon was planning the return to the Philippines, the archives provided 150 Spanish-made maps that the United States had acquired during the war with Spain in 1898.

The archives also contain information that can be vital to persons who need to prove their citizenship, to confirm land titles or to provide various kinds of legal evidence. Take the case of a Japanese-American man in California who wanted to enter college, but was unable to produce his high school diploma. He had been interned in a relocation center during World War II, and had attended a school no longer in existence. The archives unearthed his record in the files of a defunct agency and mailed him a transcript.

The Federal Register Division publishes and makes available to the public the daily *Federal Register,* which includes presidental proclamations and executive orders; the Federal regulations and the U.S. statutes-at-large, laws and regulations under which we all live. In addition, it compiles and publishes the *Government Organization Manual,* a volume familiar to most high school students.

Office of the Presidential Libraries. The Franklin D. Roosevelt Library, established in 1939, administers the papers and collections of the late president. At present there are five other presidential libraries in various parts of the country and in varying stages of development.

National Library of Medicine

Originally known as the Library of the Surgeon General's Office, this library began as a collection of 3,000 volumes in 1836. From 1865 to 1895, when Dr. John Shaw Billings was librarian, it was developed as a national resource. In 1956, after several name changes, it became the National Library of Medicine, an independent unit of the Public Health Service. By 1965 it had become the world's largest research library in a single scientific and professional field, with holdings of well over a million items in more than 70 languages.

As the world's largest biomedical library, N.L.M. considers that it has the responsibility for the comprehensive indexing of the world's literature in medicine and biology. To serve the world's biomedical community, N.L.M. has for many years published subject indexes, the best known of which is *Index Medicus,* begun in 1879.

Because of the tremendous growth of biomedical literature, N.L.M. has developed MEDLARS, previously mentioned in connection with technology and cooperative patterns. The Medical Literature Analysis and Retrieval System joins the skills of trained analysts to the processing capabilities of an electronic computer. The literature analysts review each article and decide how it should be indexed. This data is punched on tapes, put into the computer and transferred to magnetic tape for storage and retrieval.

N.L.M. is organized into seven divisions:

> Technical Services
> Reference Services
> Bibliographic Services
> Data Processing
> History of Medicine
> Publications and Translations
> Research and Training

The Research and Training Division is of particular importance to anyone interested in the field. It fosters programs to train specialists and makes available training grants and traineeships in the fields of medical librarianship, biomedical science and related subjects.

From time to time announcements of such grants are

sent to college libraries and large public libraries. Or write to the library itself at 8600 Wisconsin Ave., Bethesda, Md.

National Library of Agriculture

Established in 1862 as part of the Department of Agriculture, 100 years later it became a national library. Today its 1,500,000 volumes include not only books but journals, reports and pamphlets from more than 200 countries in some 50 languages.

It serves the Washington and field staff of the department, and makes its resources available to research workers and to the general public. World-wide in scope, its collection covers all aspects of agriculture and related biological and chemical sciences, agricultural engineering and marketing research, rural sociology and storage of farm products and home economics. In 1964 a special information center on pesticides was founded; in this specialized collection is an all-important section on man and natural resources. With catastrophe threatening the world because of too many people, too little food and too much pollution, researchers all over the globe are making increased use of this national library.

Other Government Libraries

Although making extensive use of the Library of Congress, each branch of the government has its own library. Both the Senate and the House of Representatives have specialized collections, as does the Supreme Court and the Tax Court of the United States.

In the Executive Branch, each department has a highly specialized collection whose specific purpose is to serve the department's programs. To mention just a few: the Department of Commerce maintains a large general library and the specialized Bureau of the Census Library, the Patent Office Scientific Library and the Weather Bureau Library.

As first Secretary of State, Thomas Jefferson established the Department of State Library in 1789. Today, about one third of its large collection consists of publications in foreign languages. It also serves the many embassies and consulates around the globe. More than one adventurous librarian has worked his way around the world with the help of State Department Libraries.

Many independent government agencies also have their own libraries. The Civil Aeronautics Board, the Federal Communications Commission, the National Labor Relations Board, the Securities and Exchange Commission—all have their own highly specialized collections.

Such libraries vary in size and scope, but most are small and limited to agency programs. A few, however, have extensive collections to back up more extensive activities: the FBI, the CIA and the Bureau of the Budget.

And, finally, there are the Smithsonian Institution libraries, with their wealth of scientific and technical literature. Although part of its collection is deposited with the Library of Congress, much of it remains in special libraries.

All of these are individual libraries, tailored to meet the needs of a special and limited clientele. But there are also government-supported library systems, both in the United States and overseas—those located on the NASA installations, for example.

One of the smaller systems is that of the Federal Reserve Board, with the main library in Washington and 12 branches across the country. Used by the bank's economists and other banks, the collections include pertinent government reports and publications, as well as all types of economic material. As statistical data comprise a large part of these collections, the librarians need a working knowledge of statistical methods and interpretation, the type of knowledge you would acquire as an economics major.

One of the largest systems is that of the Veteran's Administration. In Washington it operates two central libraries, the Law Library and the Medical and General Reference Library. Each installation also operates two libraries, a general one for the patients and a medical one for the staff. Professional librarians are on duty at all installations, a generalist for the patients' library and a specialist for the medical one.

By far the largest system is the world-wide network managed by the Department of Defense—"the biggest business in the world" in the words of one library director.

The Army Library Program had its origin back in the time of the Civil War, when wooden cases containing 125 books were shipped to training camps and rest centers. Until World War II the program was primarily recreational and manned by untrained personnel. During World War II it was greatly expanded and became an educational as well as a recreational service, with a staff of trained librarians.

The library on an Army installation means many things to the men in uniform. It is an information center for the commander and his staff, a technical or special library for the specialist. It is also a public library for all military personnel and their families. It is often a cultural center as well, putting on forums or music hours.

In recent years colleges and universities have begun to offer courses on military posts, or by correspondence. There are more than 25,000 soldier-scholars scattered around the world. As a result, the post librarian often doubles as a college librarian, selecting materials needed for courses of all kinds.

In addition to the post libraries, there are those in hospitals which bring books directly to bed patients. There are also bookmobiles and field collections to bring materials to men who are on maneuvers or stationed in outposts or at forward areas. All told, there are today over 1,000 library units in the Army Library Program.

All Army librarians are civilian employees, the majority in the Federal Civil Service. The staffs in the more than 460 post libraries vary from two librarians and one assistant to ten librarians and 30 nonprofessionals in the large libraries, such as Fort Bragg, N.C.

Not only is the Army Library Program the largest in the world, but it has been a technological pioneer. Many of the innovations being adopted by large and specialized libraries were pioneered by Army libraries.

Although not so extensive, the number of personnel to be served not being so large, the other services have comparable programs. The Navy operates general libraries at stations ashore and aboard ship. The Air Force provides library service for its personnel, whether they be stationed at Edwards Air Force Base in the California desert, in frigid Iceland or in the tropics.

USIS (United States Information Service), libraries make up another overseas system. It began during World

War II with a group of 35 libraries, most of them in the British Commonwealth. By 1967 USIS was operating 152 libraries in 81 countries.

These libraries were originally established to tell the story of the United States abroad, but the underlying philosophy has changed and broadened. No longer merely a window *on* the United States, the libraries aim to build a common understanding *between* the United States and other countries—in other words, to build international understanding.

Each library, by law, must have on its shelves information about the United States, and must have available different points of view on national and international issues. Aside from these requirements, each collection is tailored to the interests of its particular public. Today about 30 per cent of the books are in the local language or dialect; for example, one of this writer's children's books—*Willy Wong, American*—was translated into Marathi for use in the Bombay library.

Nonprint as well as printed materials are available in all libraries. To reach a larger audience, especially in countries where few speak or read English, more than books are needed. All USIS librarians plan and present special programs—film showings and concerts of recorded music, lectures and discussion groups, exhibits, programs for children, even English lessons.

Less well known is another activity of USIS librarians. In the United States we take for granted a community library with open bookshelves free to all citizens. But in many countries where the public library is in its infancy these are startling new ideas. So USIS librarians do all they can to help their local colleagues by providing materials and advice, often arranging for workshops.

From the beginning the USIS libraries have been on the political firing line. First, at home, there were anti-Communist hearings led by the late Senator Joseph McCarthy. Charges were made that the overseas collections included books by authors who were Communist sympathizers. These charges led to cuts in funds and a decrease in the number of libraries.

This setback damaged but did not destroy the overseas libraries. In recent years they have grown, slowly but steadily, in number and in size—and in influence. On the official level they are recognized as an imaginative and invaluable aid in building international understanding. The man in the street testifies to their value by waiting in line for the door to open.

And yet, when political turmoil spills over into the streets, USIS libraries are often stoned or burned. In Algiers, where windows and furniture were smashed and materials ruined, ultraconservative Frenchmen launched the attack. Why? Because they felt that U.S. policy favored Arab nationalism. In Athens and Cairo, in Turkey and Indonesia, among other places, USIS libraries have been primary targets. A strange kind of proof, but proof nonetheless, that they have made their presence felt. The USIS libraries, and their librarians, are involved in the making of history. They are where the international action is.

A Summing Up

A civil service announcement, *Opportunities for Librarians in the Federal Service,* gives this summary of the many choices available in government-supported libraries:

"Librarian positions in the Federal career service are located in a variety of different types of Government libraries or other information facilities. . . . Federal libraries may operate as (a) general libraries, (b) research libraries, (c) special (or technical) libraries, or (d) academic libraries. . . . In short, the Federal librarian has many career opportunities to utilize both his professional background in library science and his subject knowledge and skills."

STATE LIBRARIES

In 1811 Massachusetts began a program whereby various states exchanged the laws of their annual legislatures. By 1876 every state and territory had started a similar collection. Each of these governmental libraries collected and preserved all the official publications of its own area and, in so far as possible in those pioneer times, those of other states and territories. In addition, they assembled materials in American history, especially those pertaining to the particular region. It was these documents which formed the foundations of today's state libraries.

Located in the capitol, the library serves state officials and agencies. Its librarians provide the legislature, the courts, the departments and agencies with legal information, with any and all information as needed and with bibliographies and abstracts. They may also help to organize small, specialized collections for departments and agencies.

What specific services does a state library provide? At the Connecticut State Library on a typical day there were phone calls from the Governor's office about developing an oral history program; a member of the Gen-

eral Assembly concerning improved legislative reference
service; a reporter wanting to know why the library had
refused to approve the site of his town's new library; the
Secretary of State's office inquiring about the display of
the state's new constitution; and a distant library trustee
upset because the town's new mayor wanted to fire the
librarian. There was mail concerning the cost of cen-
tralized processing, ideas for Federal project grants and
the hiring of a consultant for the state law libraries.
There were conferences with the staff, about the teletype
network for interlibrary loans; the state library association, about grants-in-aid; and the Examiner of Public
Records, about a newly authorized department of archives.

Over the years state libraries have developed other
functions, among them an extension service. To extend
means to stretch out, to widen or enlarge. State libraries
have indeed stretched out, across fields and deserts and
up to mountaintops, to bring books to people in towns
and hamlets with no libraries. They have stretched out
to reach into prisons and into hospitals; in some states
they distribute Library of Congress materials for the
blind.

For years state libraries did all this in the face of over-
whelming odds. All too often, as legislatures passed laws
to create new services, they neglected to provide funds.
And these multiple activities were carried out on shoe-
string budgets. During the Depression of the 1930s such
programs were among the first to be cut back, if not
eliminated. During World War II both funds and personnel were in critically short supply. In some communities only the actions of civic-minded citizens or organizations kept libraries open at all. At the same time, state

libraries were called upon to expand services to hospitals and military camps and to provide the civilian population with information and materials about the war.

When the profession took stock at the conclusion of the war, it was estimated that some 33,000,000 people had no free library service. Clearly, the "big-brother approach"—doling out help in a limited, haphazard way—was not going to suffice.

To remedy the situation, the American Library Association, working with state and other national organizations, spearheaded a drive to get the Public Library Demonstration Bill through Congress. It failed to pass—by three votes. When a library assistance bill finally did pass, the state library ceased to be a big brother and became big business.

As one state librarian said: "The role of the director of a state library agency changed from that of big brother with a small agency budget to an administrative and management post calling for the wisdom of Solomon, the patience of Job, the financial wizardry of Bernard Baruch and a general know-how about data processing and complex information retrieval systems."

The responsibilities of the state library are awesome. To mention a few of long-range importance, it must:

Conduct research to determine public library needs.
Prepare an estimate of money needed to support a proposed program.
Provide consultants for and participate in the development of all types of libraries (urban as well as those in sparsely settled areas with which state libraries have traditionally worked).
Develop standards for grants-in-aid and administer such grants.

In short, the state library has a dual role—to function as a clearinghouse and to provide leadership. If the responsibilities of the state libraries have been awesome, their recent achievements have been impressive.

In some states extension services have been established; in others existing programs have been expanded. New county and regional systems have been developed; workshops and institutes have helped to train new workers and to update procedures in smaller libraries. During the first few years of Federal programs, field personnel was doubled throughout the United States with more than 200 professional librarians added to state library staffs. A number of states have developed scholarship programs to combat the lack of trained librarians. Millions of books and other materials have been put in circulation, hundreds of bookmobiles on the road.

More recently, the emphasis has been on developing and coordinating interlibrary cooperation. Michigan, for example, launched a program whose objective was "good library service within the reach of every resident of Michigan." A "hot line" to speed up reference service began operation in 1964. Over it come requests for specialized information from 19 newly organized library systems serving more than 5,000,000 people. If materials are not available in the state library, they are loaned by some other library. After only two months of daily contact with the state library, one of the systems found its headquarters so deluged with requests that it added another reference librarian.

What of the future?

There are two things to keep in mind.

First: the agency which performs library services varies from state to state. In one it may be a state library, in another a division of the Department of Education. As the organization differs, so too may the philosophy and the range of activities. So you will need to investigate how *your* state library functions and know the scope of its activities.

Whatever the governmental structure, however, librarians will be needed to continue—and expand—these departments and services:

> General reference, with increasing demand
> as cooperative patterns develop
> Legal and legislative reference
> Government documents collection and reference
> The state's historical section
> Extension agency
> Special collections (materials for the blind,
> prints, etc.)
> All technical services, on an increasing
> scale.

Second: funds available at the time you finish library school. Again, states differ, and in each state each legislature may differ: one session may be generous, another stingy. At the Federal level, in 1966 Congress extended the Library Services and Construction Act for five years, which means that the 1970s may well see changes as administrations vary. During this decade, therefore, state library services may remain stationary; they may be curtailed, or they may be expanded.

Almost certainly, however, state libraries will continue to stimulate the efforts of all types of libraries to serve their communities better. With the help of the new technology, they will coordinate the resources of these libraries to make information available to all citizens.

And state libraries will continue to work behind the scenes as the librarian's library.

As a Missouri State Library advertisement put it:

> Want to be where the ACTION is? Want an opportunity to help develop innovative programs to serve STATE GOVERNMENT? Interested in libraries(ians) and their future in today's society? . . .

FOR MORE INFORMATION

Gates, Jean Key. *Introduction to Librarianship.* McGraw-Hill, New York: 1968. Chap. 13: Federal libraries. Chap. 14: state libraries.

Wilson Library Bulletin, April, 1968. Issue devoted to the role of the state librarian.

VII

SPECIAL LIBRARIES

For the Particular Needs and Interests
of Organizations and Researchers

ORIGIN AND DEVELOPMENT

The collection of a special library is one with some common characteristic. Perhaps it is science—the Crerar collection in Chicago; or witchcraft, at Harvard. It may be an author—the Keats or Dante collections, also at Harvard. Or it can be a place of origin—the incomparable manuscripts in Istanbul; publications of the Confederate states in this country.

The earliest special libraries in the United States were those established by the historical societies in the Eastern states. Later, as pioneers moved west across the county, similar groups and collections were formed. Without these special libraries many records of our early history would in all likelihood have vanished forever.

In the 1820s, law firms began to organize their own collections of reference and research materials. In the latter half of the century, endowed research libraries began to appear. Not only Andrew Carnegie but many of the magnates of that era were interested in books and libraries. Railroad tycoon Henry E. Huntington is sup-

An early library.

The New York Public Library bookmobile in 1932.

The main branch of the New York Public Library.

The Lincoln Center Library and Museum of the Performing
Arts, a branch of the New York Public Library.

The modern library serves people of all ages.

The California State Library Building, Sacramento.

The busy circulation desk at the California State Library.

The government publications section of the California State Library.

Term paper time at the California State Library.

The neighborhood library performs many services for the community.

This new bookmobile, owned by the California State Library, provides county-wide public library service to Nevada County.

Inside a library on wheels.

The company librarian must handle many requests for information.

The Federal Reserve Bank of San Francisco is one example of a specialized Federal library.

The Los Angeles County Law Library.

The library of the Aerospace Corporation, in Los Angeles.

The computerized reference system in the Aerospace Corporation library.

The reading room of the Gompers Junior High School Library in Madison, Wisconsin.

School children meet author Holling C. Holling and his wife.

Audiovisual materials are increasingly used in school libraries.

Students use a
filmstrip previewer
in the Central Park
Road Elementary
School Library,
Plainview, New York.

Businesses sometimes cooperate with libraries in setting up special exhibits.

posed to have commented: "The ownership of a fine library is the surest and swiftest way to immortality."

Beyond dispute, he achieved immortality with the Huntington Library and Art Gallery in San Marino, on the outskirts of Los Angeles. On permanent exhibit are materials which trace the evolution of the book and lettering from handwritten beginnings to printing. The English Literature collection includes the "First Folio" edition of *Mr. William Shakespeares Comedies, Histories & Tragedies* (London, 1623) and first editions of *Paradise Lost, Pilgrim's Progress* and *Vanity Fair.* In the Americana section is the only known copy of the first collection of the laws of an English colony, the *Lawes and Libertyes . . . of . . . Massachusetts* (Cambridge, 1648).

Endowments for special collections continued in the 20th century. In 1924 J. P. Morgan established the Pierpont Morgan Library (New York City) as a memorial to his father. It houses an outstanding collection of illuminated medieval and Renaissance manuscripts, prints and Rembrandt etchings.

In 1930 Henry Clay Folger, at one time president of Standard Oil of New York, organized one of the most important book collections on British civilization, 1485-1715. Included in it are some 145,000 volumes by and about Shakespeare and an exhibition gallery which contains a small theater patterned after a playhouse typical of the period. Scholars from all parts of the world converge on the Folger Shakespeare Library in Washington, a marble structure just north of the Library of Congress.

Around the turn of the century business and industry began to collect and organize reference and research materials. In the next 50 years the number of special libraries grew steadily. After World War II, coincident with the information explosion and technological changes, more and more organizations started their own collections. By 1965 the Special Libraries Association estimated that there were 10,000 such collections; in the 1968-69 *American Library Directory* the grand total was 27,746.

There are independent specialized libraries, more than 4,000 of them, and more than 1,100 separate subject collections in college and university systems. Subject departments of large public libraries and on armed forces installations number almost 500. There are over 1,100 medical, 488 law and 550 religious libraries, to which must be added the specialized collections on many campuses.

So great has been the growth of special collections that there is now a separate directory, *Directory of Special Libraries and Information Centers*. It lists more than 13,000 sources of specialized information in libraries, information and documentation centers in the United States and Canada providing information in depth on more than 2,000 subjects. In addition, the *Research Centers Directory* describes 4,500 institutes and laboratories, both independent and university-sponsored.

NEEDED: FACTS AND FIGURES

In Aerospace

"The clock is running—four, three, two, one, zero. Liftoff!"

When you watch a space launch and astronauts moving about on the moon, do you ever think about all the people who have contributed to these spectacular achievements? The aerospace librarian is one of the behind-the-scenes workers who has helped to make dramatic advances in space science possible.

Aerospace Corporation in California, for example, provides information on tracking and telemetry, orbits, rendezvous and docking, re-entry vehicles, manned and unmanned systems, space physics and aerodynamics, management and systems-planning engineering. As Lockheed moved into outer space it developed a Missiles and Space Division, which has its own Technical Information Center. And Hughes Aircraft has no less than seven highly specialized collections.

Taming the growing information giant requires professional skill and ingenuity. Some aerospace librarians use elaborate computerized systems to cope with the immense volume of technical data required by their highly specialized patrons. Others work with more traditional techniques.

Perhaps the importance of the library is indicated by its position at one of the newer installations. A separate building, it is in the center of the complex.

In Business

The business library is to corporations and companies what a public library is to a community—an information center, a place to consult current statistical releases and forecasts, domestic and foreign documents, books and newspapers, trade magazines. Business librarians work with executives, analysts, management personnel, salesmen—all kinds of businessmen who need specialized information to help in day-to-day operations and to plan for future projects.

Libraries vary in size and scope according to the size and scope of a firm's operations. General Motors' extensive collection includes engineering, automotive history and industry, labor relations and legal materials. Eastman Kodak has organized its library into separate collections: apparatus and optical division, color technology library, a business library and the research library. Over the years the large oil companies have developed extensive geology collections. Banks with world-wide interests need statistical material from the United Nations and foreign countries. A library in one of the World Trade Centers collects directories and telephone books from Anchorage, Alaska, to Zurich, Switzerland.

Whatever the subject of the collection, it will include directories, statistical data, annual reports and newsletters, as well as books and journals. The librarian in business and industry, in finance and banking must know the collection thoroughly. He must be able to find the needed facts and figures—quickly. At the ring of the telephone, he may be asked to provide information about:

the demographic breakdown of several small towns in an area
the address of an electronic parts manufacturer in Denmark
the number of tugboats in an American port
the daily newspapers in several countries having English editions.

The business librarian must also have the imagination and the background knowledge to be able to predict what information will be needed in the future. Having material on hand, ready for use when needed, is an important part of any business library service.

In Medicine

The doctor, the research scientist, the student—each needs the most up-to-date information in his field. The medical librarian provides the link between the scientist and the information—information that is changing and growing at an explosive rate.

The medical librarian may be called upon to:

locate specific information for a surgeon
lecture about the resources of the library to a class of
    student nurses
translate an article from a foreign journal for an intern
prepare a bibliography for a research unit.

Whenever an article by a staff member is published, or a local conference held, it is almost certain that the medical librarian has contributed.

Medical libraries vary in size from the National Library of Medicine, with the largest collection in the world, to highly specialized libraries with 5,000 or less. Most collections have from 20,000 to 75,000 volumes.

The small libraries may not be directly concerned with mechanization and computerization. But the larger ones —in medical centers, universities, the pharmaceutical industry and government agencies—are very much concerned with automatic data processing and information retrieval. Only in this way can they hope to cope with the deluge of medical information.

The development of large regional information storage and retrieval systems has created a critical manpower shortage. Information system specialists and professionally trained administrative personnel are urgently needed to manage complex libraries and information systems.

To meet this need a two-year master's degree in library administration has been developed (funded by the U.S. Public Health Service and administered by the National Library of Medicine). There is also a federally funded, in-service training program (a library degree plus one year).

If you want more information about the practically unlimited career opportunities in the field of medical librarianship, write:

Executive Secretary
Medical Library Association, Inc.
919 North Michigan Ave.
Chicago, Ill. 60611

Not to be confused with the medical librarian is the medical record librarian. As the title indicates, medical record librarians prepare and maintain medical and surgical records on patients. In large hospitals the staff consists of a chief librarian, who supervises other librarians, technicians and clerks. In such institutions medical record librarians may do more than keep important records. They may compile statistics and make abstracts, analyze records and reports, assist the medical staff in research projects. In a small hospital, on the other hand, there may be only one such employee, and he may perform clerical as well as professional duties.

The increasing number of hospitals, together with the volume and complexity of medical records, has created a growing demand for those qualified in the field. To qualify, you need a certificate from one of the schools approved by the American Medical Association; by 1966 there were 28 such schools located in colleges and universities as well as in hospitals. Wherever this specialized training, about a year in length, is offered, the curriculum is about the same. But the prerequisites vary, ranging from two to four years of college-level work, with the latter increasingly preferred.

For more information about this growing specialization, write:

American Association of Medical Record Librarians
840 North Lake Shore Drive
Chicago, Ill. 60611

In the Arts

Art librarians are very privileged persons. During their working hours they are surrounded by beauty; their tools are handsome books, prints, and reproductions, color slides. They usually work in pleasant surroundings, in museums or galleries, in a department library on campus or a design center. Their patrons are artists and scholars, art collectors and dealers. If they enjoy working under pressure, there are advertising and publishing collections. If they prefer working with many types of people, there are the art departments of the public libraries.

There have long been music and theater collections. And as motion pictures developed, so too did their libraries. For the most part, they developed in the studios when the big spectaculars—requiring research for costumes, sets and so on—were at their height. Today films, for theaters and television, are in a state of transition. And the libraries, most of them with smaller staffs, are marking time. Whatever the future of the commercial film—and certainly in this audiovisual age it has a future—there will have to be libraries to meet its very special requirements.

In the past, libraries serving the arts have been individual units. But something new has recently happened. In New York's Lincoln Center there is the Library and Museum of the Performing Arts. It combines the usual functions of a library and a museum. But the way in which these functions have been brought together is unique. Since the performing arts are to be seen and heard, the library has made imaginative use of audiovisual devices. One of the first things to meet the eye of the visitor is a kaleidoscope of music, dance, opera, the theater and the circus, puppetry and magic. Projected on a 21-inch screen, the changing scenes show the variety of the performing arts, their blending, the likenesses that tie them together. Attached to the general library is a 200-seat auditorium. In addition, there are smaller rooms with film projectors but no stages. And the children have their own theater in the center of the children's library.

For professionals—composers, choreographers, actors, designers, and writers—Lincoln Center has a research library, with its specialized collections.

> Music . . . the largest in the country outside of the Library of Congress.
>
> Theater . . . contains some record of every play produced in New York City in the last 100 years.
>
> Motion Picture . . . contains reviews of every film released since 1930.
>
> Dance . . . the first in the world devoted exclusively to the subject.

This library-museum may be unique now, but the concept behind it may be the wave of the future.

Fields of the Future

Oceanography. There are already several collections in existence. The Woods Hole Oceanographic Institute, in Massachusetts, has a document library well under way, and several universities are building collections. One of these, at the University of Southern Califorina, started out as a biology library which has long been regarded as priceless by scholars throughout the world. As oceanography began to emerge as a science, this library broadened its scope to become the Hancock Library of Biology and Oceanography. As scientists began to explore the sea, the literature began to grow, so much so that there is now an Oceanic Index and Oceanic Abstracts. The 80,000-volume U.S.C. collection brings together related materials in the fields of zoology, fisheries, geology and botany to provide scholars and scientists information in depth. The 1970s will probably see oceanography collections grow, and new ones appear, as knowledge of the field expands.

Ecology. Belatedly, man has come to realize that science and technology may be creating an environment in which he cannot survive. As society begins to tackle this potential disaster, information is scattered far and wide in separate collections. If we are to avoid catastrophe, the library world will have to assemble materials from many disciplines so that the experts, government agencies and the general public can get at the information necessary to develop new outlooks, to coordinate new policies. What form the library's contribution will take is unclear.

But it is clear that in the next decade the library world will be involved in making that necessary information available. Environmental control is a field that will be needing librarians and information specialists.

THE SPECIALIST'S SPECIALIST

According to the *Dictionary of Occupational Titles,* the special librarian "is a trained professional who serves as the link between the informational writer and publisher and the users of the information. Whereas the general library may deal with written materials of a broad and general nature, the Special Librarian, sometimes called a 'specialist's specialist,' obtains, handles, stores, categorizes, analyzes, and makes available information of a specific nature covering a specific field or area. His or her services are now in demand by government and industry, and by medical, communication, business and other groups who need and seek library information peculiar to their fields."

In simpler language, the special librarian puts knowledge to work for a special clientele. Whether his library is in an aerospace center or a bank, a hospital or an oil company, it is the information nerve center of the organization. And it might be pointed out that the dictionary is behind the times—these days a special library often contains audiovisual as well as "written materials."

What, exactly, does a special librarian do? Everything.

He plans the physical arrangement of the collection; organizes the reference materials; selects and purchases books, journals, documents and nonprint materials; and supervises the classification and cataloging of books and indexes other materials. This requires imagination and inventiveness; the collection and arrangement must be adapted to the particular needs of the organization.

The special librarian also supervises files of special materials, supervises reader services and handles reference requests. To take an imaginary example, suppose an engineer thinks that he has discovered a new process. To make certain that it is original he enlists the help of the company librarian, who will thoroughly investigate the known sources of information. In this case he would have to be familiar with engineering techniques because he will be referring to professional handbooks and technical research reports, scientific encyclopedias and journals, and he will have to search volumes of U.S. patents.

To cite actual requests received by the library of a gas and electric company, "simple" ones have asked for complete data on steam accumulators used in a certain plant in West Germany, information on the safe operation of interlocking systems burning pulverized fuel, oil and gas. Less routine was the rush order by the sales promotion department. Needed: one baby elephant, an attendant for same and three pistols of the type used in Vienna in 1850. The company library delivered all items by curtain time.

The special librarian reviews and abstracts current literature. This is an exceedingly important function, for busy members of busy organizations do not have the time to read all the material in their fields. But a one-paragraph abstract or review will tell them whether to read the whole article, report or book.

He makes or supervises literature searches—another very important function. One large oil company, for example, prepares a basic reading list on petroleum. This annotated list contains information basic both to the industry and to the literature of a specific field. It is for two groups of readers, those without petroleum background and petroleum specialists who need information on other parts of the industry.

The special librarian does not merely wait on his patrons. He not only obtains materials his organization already knows it needs but also searches for information it does not yet know it needs, and for this he must possess initiative and ingenuity. He is, in other words, the bibliographic brain of his organization.

And the special librarian prepares annual reports to management concerning library activities and future plans; prepares the budget; attends organization meetings, research conferences, seminars and professional meetings; contributes to or edits organization publications (libraries of larger firms may be responsible for a daily news summary); and issues a library bulletin.

How does the organization librarian, in a private firm or government agency, differ from the specialist in a department of a public library? Both need professional skills and ingenuity, but there are several significant differences.

1. In a company or agency you work with the same people day by day, as a member of a team that is operating or developing projects. In a public library, on the other hand, your clientele is ever changing and varied.

2. The collections are different. One obvious example: the business department of a public library will provide some material on all major aspects of a subject—the library of a large insurance company, say, will have a comprehensive collection of materials related to that subject only.

3. The organization librarian usually does the cataloging and is free to experiment, to try new ideas. In a

public library this function is performed by separate departments for the whole system.

4. Working conditions differ. Most public librarians must count on night duty at least once a week and sometimes on Saturdays. Most special librarians keep regular office hours. Salaries are somewhat higher, although the pay in public library work has increased steadily in recent years. And there are some built-in hazards to keep in mind. In a business slowdown the library is as subject to layoffs as the assembly line. If the firm, whether it is doing research or making space hardware, is operating under contract to the Federal Government, cutbacks by an economy-minded Congress reach into the library.

You do not have to be a specialist to be a special librarian. But, increasingly, some degree of specialization—knowledge of a specific field and its techniques—will prove an asset. Witness some recent advertisements. A major oil company seeking a librarian to direct information services at one of its technical centers advertised: "An undergraduate degree in chemistry or chemical engineering is preferred, and proficiency in information retrieval techniques is highly desirable." The U.S. Geological Survey Library stated: "Candidates should possess broad academic knowledge of earth sciences. . . ."

FOR MORE INFORMATION

Read the professional journal *Special Libraries*.
Write to:
    Special Libraries Association
    31 East 10th Street
    New York, N.Y. 10003

Executive Secretary
Medical Library Association, Inc.
919 North Michigan Ave.
Chicago, Ill. 60611

American Association of Law Libraries
50 West Jackson Blvd.
Chicago, Ill. 60604

VIII

LIBRARIES ON CAMPUS

IN THE BEGINNING

Before the American Revolution, any institution of learning beyond high school was known as a college. Shortly after the Revolution, state universities began to appear, but so meager was their financial support that they were, in effect, mediocre public colleges. Not until 1825, when Jefferson established the University of Virginia, did the country have a public institution that offered more advanced work than the private colleges. During the same period, some of these colleges expanded or reorganized to become universities. By the time the Civil War engulfed the nation there were 21 state universities and about 500 colleges (less than half of which survived).

Two years after it came into existence, in 1636, Harvard laid the foundation for what was to become one of the world's great libraries. In his will John Harvard left half of his property and all of his library, between 300 and 400 volumes, to the college in Cambridge. During these early years libraries at the academic institutions imposed rules and regulations calculated to discourage all but the most determined of students. At Dartmouth, for example, the library was open for one hour once every two weeks, and only five students at a time were permitted on the premises. Once inside, freshmen could take out only one book at a time, sophomores and juniors two and seniors a grand total of three. The librarians were usually faculty members, sometimes even the president himself.

Under these circumstances academic libraries were used mainly by the faculty, very little by students. In all probability only the exceptional student craved access to the library. This was because the pattern of instruction consisted of assignments in textbooks and recitation, a pattern which created no demand for adequate library facilities. Nor was a student apt to think of the library as a pleasant place to study. Dusty, poorly lighted and usually unheated, it was as devoid of creature comforts as a mausoleum.

In the latter part of the 19th century, however, the educational pattern began to change. Lectures and the German research method replaced textbook assignments and reciting in classes. As students began to study subjects, not chapters in texts, the need for better libraries and adequate access to them grew. By the turn of the century, libraries had come to be considered of pivotal importance in higher learning. And the position of librarian had become a full-time occupation. Attitudes toward the use of library resources were also changing. No longer were books hoarded, regarded as treasures to be guarded but not touched. Rather, they were made increasingly available to students and faculty alike.

TODAY AND TOMORROW

Today the campus library is one of several key factors considered in accrediting a college or university. Most catalogs indicate the number of volumes in the general library, as well as any special features of the collection and what specialized libraries are on campus. *American Universities and Colleges,* a standard reference work, includes library resources of each institution: over-all holdings, the annual budget, special collections and what arrangements exist for borrowing materials from other institutions.

The 1968 *Statistical Abstract of the United States* estimated that, as of 1967, there were 2,374 institutions of higher learning in the country. All would have at least one library; a large university would have between 15 and 20.

COLLEGES AND UNIVERSITIES

How do colleges and universities differ? Both are institutions of higher learning, but there are fundamental differences—differences that influence the type of service the libraries on campus provide.

According to the Dictionary of Education:

College—1. an institution of higher education, usually offering only a curriculum in the liberal arts and sciences. . . .

2. a major division of a university comprising the various departments offering the liberal arts on non-professional subjects.

> University—an institution of higher education, con-
> sisting of a liberal arts college, offering
> a program of graduate study, and hav-
> ing usually two or more professional
> schools or faculties and empowered to
> confer degrees in various fields of study.

As far as campus libraries are concerned, what do these distinctions mean? Both perform all of the standard library functions: selection, ordering and cataloging of materials, and reference work. Both serve a specific community, composed of students and faculty. Both support the over-all programs offered on campus. But because the college community and program differ from those of a university, the library resources and services also differ.

Number of Libraries

> College—Usually one, with a collection that serves
> as "the central intellectual resources" (in
> the words of the *Standards for College Li-
> braries*).
> University—A cluster of several libraries: a central one
> —two if there is a separate one for under-
> graduates—and smaller, highly specialized
> collections primarily for graduate students
> and researchers.

Staff

> College—Generalists (some subject specialization an
> asset), as librarians select and dispense in-

formation on a wide range of subjects, everything from art to zoology.

University—Subject specialists for the special libraries; language specialists; generalists for the central research collection.

Community Served

College—Entering freshmen to professors engaged in research.

University—Undergraduate and graduate students; faculty and research specialists.

Relation with Students and Faculty

College—Work with students to provide needed materials and to develop good habits of study and research. Work with faculty to build the collection in support of the general program and subject majors, and to assist with research.

University—Less contact with the students as, in theory, they have already developed study and research skills. Close cooperation with the faculty at all levels and in each of the schools or colleges that together comprise the university.

If the prospect of working in a college or university library appeals to you, keep these basic differences in mind as you plan your undergraduate program. Once again, you will need to decide whether you prefer to be a generalist or a specialist.

The opportunities in the special libraries on a large

university campus are many and varied. A list of those at U.C.L.A. indicates the number and range of subjects:

Architecture and Urban Planning	English Reading Room
	Geology-Geophysics
Art	Law
Biomedical	Map
Business Administration	Music
Chemistry	Oriental
Education and Psychology	Physics
	Theater Arts
Engineering and Mathematical Sciences	University Elementary School

In addition, several other departments maintain special collections: Biophysics and Nuclear Medicine, Mathematics, the Neuropsychiatric Institute. And, finally, there is one off-campus library with rare collections of English culture, covering the period 1640-1750, and of Montana history.

At other universities there are collections reflecting areas of special concern: transportation, world affairs, oceanography—name a specialized area of study, and there is probably a special library on some campus. Many valuable private collections are eventually administered and maintained by institutions of higher learning. At Smith College, for example, you will find the Einstein collection of transcripts of 16th- and 17th-century madrigal and instrumental music.

Many universities have developed a corps of bibliographers, who are responsible for building collections in specialized subject areas. The role of such specialized bibliographers is increasingly important as the world struggles to cope with the information explosion.

College and especially university libraries have promoted experimental programs concerned with the storage and retrieval of information, many in cooperation with the national libraries. In the decades ahead, campus libraries will undoubtedly continue to work on ways and means of adapting technology to library requirements.

Knowledge now comes in many nonbook forms, and campus libraries are in the process of becoming multimedia resource centers. Programmed materials, tapes and recordings—all manner of audiovisual materials—must be collected, stored and found.

It is impossible to predict what changes will occur in campus libraries during the 1970s. But it is possible to predict one thing—there will be changes, many and far-reaching.

JUNIOR COLLEGES

The American junior college is frequently called "the big discovery of the age." This is more than a public relations slogan, for both its growth and significance have been spectacular.

Forerunners of the junior colleges were private two-year institutions, the two-year curriculum of some normal schools and technical and business colleges. In 1900 there were only eight private junior colleges, and in the following year the first public one opened in Joliet, Illinois. By 1969 there were approximately 1,000 junior colleges, and the prediction for 1973 is 1,250.

What has caused this phenomenal growth? For one thing, the ever-rising number of high school graduates who want and need more education. Allied to this is the conviction that more education equals higher earning power in a technological society which has created many new jobs that require specialized skills or retraining for already existing ones. For another thing, overcrowding and rising costs at the four-year institutions have forced many students to seek further education elsewhere. While attending a low fee community college they can continue to live at home, and then transfer to a four-year college or university (about one third do transfer).

And, finally, the junior college is particularly well suited to help students from disadvantaged areas who need to acquire skills and knowledge to cope with this technological age. As the name implies, a community college may be in an inner city or near an industrial district, in a suburb or a rural region. In other words, junior colleges are within commuting distance of most of the poor seeking a way out of poverty. Furthermore, the "open door" admission policy makes it easy to get into a junior college. Financially, junior college is within reach of almost everyone. Not only is tuition low or non-existent, but extensive evening programs make it possible for students to work while studying (twice as many students attend classes at night as in the daytime).

A multipurpose institution, the junior college serves many segments of its community. It provides a general education for those who may go on to a four-year institution. It provides vocational and technical skills and semiprofessional knowledge. In addition, many two-year colleges offer adult education of whatever kind the particular community wants and needs.

The role of the library, if it is to meet the requirements of such a multipurpose institution, is a formidable one. The collection, of all types of materials, should be as broad as the course offerings—and that is very broad indeed. It should provide professional materials for the faculty, some of whom are off-campus specialists. It should provide recreational materials—for viewing and listening, as well as reading—for both students and faculty. The emphasis in most junior college libraries is on multimedia, not merely printed materials; librarians are frequently referred to as "media specialists."

Increased attention is being given to the development of library skills. Skills needed to continue a formal education, or to keep abreast of the ever-growing amount of information in the business and technical worlds. Increasingly, the library is accepting more responsibility toward the off-campus community, arranging cultural events and serving as a center for community affairs.

To serve such a varied public and to back up such a broad instructional program are difficult goals to achieve. And many junior college libraries are still far from reaching this goal.

Tomorrow and in the foreseeable future, the librarians will have challenging problems to tackle. Working in a junior college library will be strenuous—and stimulating.

CHANGES ON CAMPUS

Headlines in the late 1960s reflected the ferment simmering on campuses from coast to coast—ferment that swelled into demonstrations, sometimes into violence. Out of this turmoil have come changes in the academic communities. And, since the libraries are part of such communities, there have been changes there too. New collections have been organized—in Afro-American literature, for example, and in urban and environmental studies.

Less visible—you cannot see it on the shelves—but perhaps even more important, is the changing role of the campus library. Behind some of the headlines lurked student dissatisfaction with the sit-and-listen method of teaching, with the memorize-the-facts-for-exams way of learning. Even before the campus upheavals the "independent study" movement was developing. You have doubtless encountered "independent study" in the form of a term paper or research project.

Already the independent-study concept of learning is bringing about far-reaching changes in higher education—changes that directly affect the college library.

As to the future, one educator, Harold Gores, predicts: "By 1980, colleges and universities will be well on their way to becoming mostly libraries. . . . .

"Clearly, the solution will not be more buildings, more books and more librarians, but a change in the concept of what a library is. The library will cease to be a depository of books and become a source of information. . . .

"Changes in the modes of instruction will displace the classroom as the center of learning. The library will occupy its place."

And he concludes: "The dominating facilities will be the library, where the information is, and the living rooms, where the meaning of the information is determined. The library will house the facts and fancies. The living rooms, née classrooms, will provide the arena where the student, fortified with relevant information and in the company of his fellows and faculty, hammers out the values, the meaning of it all."

And what will be the role of the librarian in this trend toward independent study? It will vary, of course, as institutions of higher learning will vary in their attempts to serve their particular student and faculty communities. But two things are already clear. The library will no longer merely support and supplement classroom instruction. And the librarian will be a teacher as well as a librarian. After all, it is he who is trained to guide the undergraduate to an education in the library. At one college already well along the road to total independent study it has been found that librarians are becoming teachers and teachers are becoming librarians.

The road to 1980 is strewn with many question marks. But about one thing there is no question. It will be a period of drastic and dramatic changes. And the library and the librarian will be at the center of these changes.

FOR MORE INFORMATION

College and Research Libraries (a bimonthly magazine).

Eurich, Alvin C., ed. *Campus 1980.* New York: Delacarte Press, 1968.

Gleazer, Edmund, J., Jr., "The Stake of the Junior College in Its Libraries," *College and Research Libraries,* July, 1966.

Library Trends, July, 1969. Issue devoted to college librarianship.

Scott, W. Wiley, "The Library's Place in the Junior College," *Library Trends,* October, 1965.

Shores, Louis, "The Library College Idea," *Library Journal,* September 1, 1966.

IX

SCHOOL LIBRARIES

By the end of the 1960s there were a number of model school libraries in various sections of the country. Such a library has a carefully selected collection of the customary printed materials—books, pamphlets and magazines. In addition, it houses many nonprint materials: filmstrips and 8-mm. filmloops, slides and transparencies, slides and charts, maps and globes, art and social studies prints, programmed instructional materials. These are "model" libraries—not, unfortunately, average ones—indicative of the trend toward independent study and media centers.

Such learning centers contrast strikingly with the first musty school libraries, which were primarily storage places for collections related to English courses. Although the school library movement has been primarily a 20th-century development, it had its beginnings in the early 1800s. Bronson Alcott, the father of the author of *Little Women,* was roundly condemned for advocating that the children in his experimental school have their own juvenile library. (He also had the outrageous idea that children should be happy in school.)

In 1827 New York's governor, DeWitt Clinton, recommended to the state legislature that a small collection of books be placed in every schoolhouse. Not until 1835, however, did New York pass the first such law. And it was another 20 years before New Jersey followed suit. By 1876, 19 of the states had enacted similar legislation.

The year 1900 not only ushered in a new century, it was also the year the first trained librarian was appointed to a full-time position in a New York school. And in 1914 the American Library Association formed the School Libraries Section.

Yet, although educational leaders from the time of Horace Mann (1796-1859) urged the establishment of libraries in school districts, the movement grew at a sluggish and uneven pace. One reason, as always with a new public service, was lack of money. Often PTA groups were the only available source of funds and staff. Another reason was the school–public library relationship. Some state library extension agencies provided traveling libraries or boxes of books on long loans. And the local public library, with its children's program already functioning, supplied both materials and services.

Until the 1940s the children's librarian of a public library spent a considerable portion of her time working with and in the schools. She visited the school to help teachers select materials; she provided lists and gave lectures on books. She attended teachers' meetings to learn about the curriculum, and in many cases gave instruction in the use of the library. And she regularly conducted classroom storytelling hours. In addition, some libraries loaned classroom collections; others maintained a special reference collection for the use of school children.

In the early 1950s the public library was still providing some or all of these services. Then, because of curriculum changes and the project method of teaching, secondary schools added to their collections and enlarged their staffs.

Things were moving along steadily, if not as rapidly as both teachers and librarians would have wished. Then came 1957—the year the Russians launched Sputnik, and an educational panic followed. Students found themselves deluged with homework, and the public libraries found themselves deluged with students. The school libraries did not have enough materials to cope with the sudden demand; nor did they have enough staff to keep open the extra hours harried students had to spend in some library.

Gradually, as sanity returned, there emerged changes in education that were to have far-reaching implications for both school and public libraries. In 1959 a commission supported by the Ford Foundation issued a pamphlet by J. Lloyd Trump, *Images of the Future*, a new approach to the secondary school. One part of the new approach was to be individual study: "Students will read, listen to records and tapes, view, question, experiment, examine, consider evidence, analyze, investigate, think, write, create, memorize, record, make, visit, and self-appraise. These activities will take place in project and materials centers, museums, workshops, libraries, and laboratories, in and outside the school."

In the years since, the trend toward independent, or individual, study and the development of learning centers has grown steadily. Junior and senior high schools throughout the country are striving to build libraries— now often called media centers—similar to the model one mentioned at the beginning of the chapter.

While these and other drastic changes have been taking place in junior and senior high schools, what has been happening in the elementary grades? Not enough. In 1964 not nearly enough, according to the Commissioner of Education, Keppel. His article in the November issue of *McCall's* magazine, "Schools Without Libraries," pointed to two alarming statistics: 60 per cent of our elementary schools, with 10,000,000 pupils, had no libraries at all; 80 per cent had no trained librarians to serve their students. And this, he reminded the readers, was the age when lifetime habits and attitudes toward reading are created.

Several years later, school librarians and audiovisual educators working together published new standards for media centers. According to these standards, the ratio should be one media specialist to 250 pupils. Yet in the prosperous state of California the 1965-66 ratio was one to 5,436 in the elementary grades and one to 1,439 in the secondary schools.

Such statisticts do not lie, but they do not tell the whole story either. In spite of these dismal figures, much has been and is being done to upgrade existing libraries and establish new ones.

During the 1962 National Library Week the Sunday supplement *This Week* ran an article on the plight of school libraries and the possibility of "demonstration" programs. The Knapp Foundation became interested and, working with the American Association of School Librarians, provided funds for such demonstration centers.

What are demonstration libraries? They test new materials and equipment, and try out new ways of working with teachers and pupils. Librarians in them are multimedia specialists, skilled in the use of all kinds of print and nonprint materials.

Cooperating closely with teacher education institutions, these projects have developed learning centers to serve an entire school community—supervisors and administrators as well as teachers and students. They have experimented with the improved-upon instructional materials for the use of all schools in planning or upgrading their own libraries.

The Knapp School Libraries Project consisted of three phases:

1963. Two programs in elementary schools with existing provisions for library service.

1964. Three programs in elementary schools in different geographic areas with less adequate library service.

1965. Three programs in secondary schools with average or above-average library service.

Also in 1965, Congress passed the Elementary and Secondary Education Act. Included in it were provisions for assistance to school library programs, the most far-reaching of which were:

1. A five-year program of financial grants for the purchase of books, including textbooks, and other instructional materials for the use of students and teachers, and for both public and private schools, from the elementary grades through high school.

2. Funds to establish supplementary edu-

cation centers, including model ones, with various types of materials, in elementary schools.

3. Funds for research in the area where service has been the weakest, the elementary school library.

The grants made available under this act (and others of less size and scope) were indeed impressive. In 1967, for example, approximately $160,000,000 was spent for printed materials; $53,200,000 was spent for audiovisual materials and equipment.

This massive financial transfusion greatly strengthened existing libraries, and enabled new ones to establish multimedia centers at the outset. It also exposed some shortcomings.

Where printed materials were concerned, the chronic shortage of librarians became acute. As an example, take one junior high school library. The staff consisted of one full-time trained librarian, one part-time clerk and 30 student helpers, working various hours on various days. The books were processed at the central technical facility, but when they arrived at the school the librarian had to get them into circulation. This meant, among other things, finding a place for them on already overcrowded shelves. This in turn meant discarding older volumes, and weeding (as it is called in library lingo), a task only a librarian can do. And where, with her usual hour-to-hour, day-to-day chores, was she to find the time? For months she could not find the time, and the boxes of books accumulated. Furthermore, the librarian wanted to make lists for and have consultations with the teachers, to acquaint them with the valuable additions to the collection. Again, where was she to find the time?

The obvious answer was to have an additional librarian on the staff. Presuming the money was available, either from the school district or from Federal funds, this was easier recommended than achieved. There simply were not enough school librarians.

There certainly were not enough librarians experienced in the audiovisual field. As these new materials flowed into libraries it became apparent that many librarians were ill equipped to cope with them. For the most part they had little understanding of the newer media, and some were openly hostile to the idea of anything except printed materials in a library. Furthermore, in older buildings facilities were inadequate to handle them.

What can be done was demonstrated by a project near Schenectady in upper New York. Using $200,000 in grants over a three-year period, the junior high school in the district transformed its library into an Environmental Learning Center, with new facilities, equipment and materials and more personnel. Students now have the use of ten study carrels, each equipped with its own video screen and earphones. To use slides and tapes, films and filmstrips or educational television programs stored in the bank of instructional materials, the student dials code numbers to indicate what he wants.

There are other, traditional carrels also available where a student can read, browse through a collection of pictures, listen to records, even play math games. In such an environment a student can pursue independent research, employ the repetitive teaching tools or just plain study.

There are multimedia carts to carry books, nonbook materials and audiovisual equipment from classroom to classroom. And the librarians work with teachers and students to plan for the use of materials for some specific lesson or project. The staff consists of three librarians (all media specialists) and three aides who work with teachers and students. In addition, there is a media production specialist.

What such a center can mean to students was described in a report from a Maine senior high school:

Before the grants were awarded, the AV equipment and materials were unorganized, uncataloged, and seldom used. Now they are in constant use, and students are benefitting from the correlation of visual and aural communications. They are learning that plays and poetry are meant to be performed and read aloud, that films about science are more effective and real to them than lectures, and that tapes of political speeches can be played again and again to reveal contradictions and weaknesses unnoticed during a first hearing. They learn to see connections and to question disparities.

These demonstration libraries represent the ideal. But they are not visionary; some are in operation, pointing the way to the future. As more and more teachers and librarians visit these centers, they return to their own schools to adapt what they have seen to their particular needs. In school districts throughout the country buildings are being renovated and remodeled. Librarians are being brought up to date by workshops, in-service training sessions and special classes.

It is not that the fundamental role of the school library has changed. It will continue to acquire, catalogue, store and retrieve the world's literature and knowledge in print. And, with the help of modern technology, it will perform the same functions for the other media. Where formerly a student could only read Hamlet's "To be or not to be" soliloquy, now he can also listen to a great actor delivering it. In other words, although the role of the school library has not changed, the role of the librarian has. And you, the future school librarians and/or media specialists, will be as skilled in the use of audiovisual materals as in the use of books.

Finally, because of the increasing emphasis on independent study, the school librarian will be at the center of the learning process, working closely with both teachers and students. How successfully he or she teaches a pupil the techniques for finding information may mean the difference between success or failure for that pupil, in college or on a job.

Proof of this generalization came from a recent Yale University report. The battery of tests given entering freshmen included one on library skills. At the end of their first year, it was found that those with the highest scores on library skills were the most successful, all-around students. In other words, to those students who arrived on campus capable of getting information on their own, using a larger and more complicated library presented no particular problems.

The school librarian will, in the future, as in the past:

Cooperate with the teachers to provide materials, of all kinds, to support and enrich the curriculum.

Work with and listen to students to offer reading, and now audiovisual, guidance.

Teach library skills.

Encourage students to explore on their own.

WHAT YOU NEED TO KNOW

Depending upon where your interest lies, in the elementary or secondary schools, you will need knowledge in the fields already mentioned in connection with work with children and young adults.

All states require that school librarians be certified. Usually, college requirements are a minimum of 15 semester hours (or the equivalent) in quarter hours of library courses. Elementary schools, in some cases, require courses in children's literature and storytelling. Since the trend is toward the requirement of a master's degree in library science, investigate thoroughly before planning your undergraduate program.

Most states also require school librarians to be certified as teachers. The number of credits in education varies from state to state, so check with the State Department of Education or with your local school superintendent. The state Education Code also includes the requirements, and there is a publication, *Requirements for Certification,* that lists by state the requirements for librarians (as well as teachers, counselors and administrators) for elementary and secondary schools and junior colleges.

FOR MORE INFORMATION

A.L.A. Bulletin, February, 1969. Includes a special section, "Educational Trends and Media Programs in School Libraries."
American Library Association. *Standards for School Media Programs,* 1969.

Audiovisual Instruction. Published monthly, except during the summer, by the National Education Association. Dedicated to the better usage of audiovisual materials, it covers all phases of this constantly expanding field.

Egan, Mary Joan. "The Library—An Environmental Learning Center," *Audiovisual Instruction,* September, 1969.

School Libraries. A quarterly magazine published by the American Association of School Librarians.

X

PREPARATION FOR A PROFESSION

Is librarianship a profession?

A brief glance backward at the development of library education may provide a partial answer to that question. The library world is indebted to Melvil Dewey for many things, among them the numerical system by which you find books on the shelves of most public and school libraries. He also advocated a program for training librarians. At first, little attention was paid to his proposals. But eventually, in 1887, he succeeded in establishing the first school for librarians: the School of Library Economy at Columbia College (it later moved to Albany and the New York State Library).

The curriculum concentrated upon the day-to-day routine functions of a library, on clerical and technical activities. It emphasized the skills and methods and ignored the principles or philosophy underlying them. In spite of its shortcomings, this first library school laid the foundation for library education. And by 1914 ten institutions of higher learning had started training programs for librarians.

Then, in 1923, came the Williamson report, a study of existing courses of study. Sharply critical of the emphasis on clerical and routine activities and the neglect of a broad general education, it signaled a turning point in library education. Mr. Williamson made some blunt statements, among them that "no amount of training in library techniques can make a successful librarian of a person who lacks a good general education." He also made certain specific recommendations which included a four-year college education (liberal arts), to be augmented by a fifth year of graduate study for professional training.

Another important development stemmed from this landmark report. Under a grant from the Carnegie Corporation the University of Chicago established a library school and launched a Ph.D. program. This program investigated fundamental problems and led to the publication of a body of professional literature that had a great impact on the entire library world. For the first time, the principles and philosophy of librarianship were examined and analyzed.

After these beginnings in the 1920s, the movement toward professional standards in librarianship gained momentum during the 1930s. World War II interrupted what had been a slow but steady growth. Then, after the war, came the information explosion and a revolution in technology—events which have posed many problems and imposed far-reaching changes.

Where does librarianship stand today? Is it a profession?

According to an abridged dictionary, a profession is an occupation requiring an education—especially law, medicine, teaching, the ministry.

To this skimpy definition the unabridged adds significant elements: a calling requiring specialized knowledge and often long and intensive instruction in skills and methods as well as the scientific, historical or scholarly principles underlying such skills and methods . . . maintains high standards of achievement and conduct, and commits its members to continued study and to a kind of work which has for its prime purpose the rendering of a public service.

How well does librarianship meet these requirements? Does it require "specialized knowledge"? Yes. Does it require "often long and intensive instruction in skills and methods"? The curriculum of most library schools covers this aspect of library science. But some schools now emphasize the theoretical, expecting the new librarian to learn many of the technical aspects on the job.

Does librarianship also require "the scientific, historical or scholarly principles underlying such skills and methods"? These were not emphasized in the past, but there is a growing awareness of the urgent need to formulate such principles. Does it "maintain high standards of achievement and conduct"? In theory, yes; in practice, not always. Does it require "continued study"? In the past, no. Today, however, it is increasingly stressed. Some library schools are already developing a continuing-education program. Does it commit its members "to a kind of work which has for its prime purpose the rendering of public service"? Yes.

There is another, simpler definition of professionalism. It holds that there are three values upon which any profession must be based:

Knowing. Systematic knowledge and intellect.
Doing. Technical skills and trained capacity.
Helping. Using knowledge and skills to serve others.

Clearly, all library work entails these basic values.

On balance, then, librarianship today may be an imperfect profession. But it is a profession hard at work trying to overcome these imperfections. Whatever its shortcomings, it is on the move. In this era of rapid change, it may not always be clear in what direction it is moving. But the momentum toward greater professionalism is strong and growing stronger.

And what does this mean as far as educational requirements are concerned? It means that to become a fully qualified librarian you will need the graduate work that is required of any profession—specifically, four years of undergraduate study, plus at least one year of specialized graduate study leading to a master's degree in library science or service. It also means that you need to plan your undergraduate program with this in mind.

UNDERGRADUATE PREPARATION

In the past, almost without exception, students planning to enter the field of librarianship took a general liberal arts course. Today many library schools recommend a different approach.

Take, for example, the advice in the catalog of the School of Library Science at Case Western Reserve University, one of the first institutions to offer a degree in librarianship:

For all students
    a sound general education
    basic knowledge of at least one foreign language
    undergraduate specialization in a field of your choice

For public library service
    undergraduate specialization in at least one of
    these fields: sociology, psychology, economics, his-
    tory or the humanities
For school librarianship
    courses in education
For college and university libraries
    more specific specialization—for example:
        in the sciences, physical or biological
        in the humanities, art or music or literature
For special libraries (other than on campus)
    sound preparation in science or social science
    subject specialization within the field, depending
        upon your interests

This more specialized approach indicates that during
your junior and senior years you should take courses in
subjects related to the library field of most interest to
you. And this, in turn, means that you have to decide
what field *does* most interest you. As with any profession,
you have to plan for it—you cannot just drift into it.

A few examples from recent advertisements in library
journals underline the necessity of planning ahead. Several university libraries included these qualifications:

Prior experience and background in physical sciences
desirable.
Prior experience, knowledge of a foreign language or
a scientific field desirable.
Science cataloger with strong science background.
Romance language cataloger.

And the Business and Economics Department of a

large public library wanted academic background in economics and/or experience with business literature.

If you are on a campus with a library school, find out if it permits students to take certain required courses during their junior and senior years. Sooner or later you will have to take basic courses in cataloging and reference sources, and the trend is to offer these prerequisites at the undergraduate level. And some schools have designated additional courses which may be taken before entering the graduate program.

ENTRANCE REQUIREMENTS . .

Library schools differ, although only slightly, in admission requirements. There are, however, certain minimum requirements common to all accredited programs:

1. A bachelor's degree from an accredited college or university.
2. Graduate Record Examination.
3. A personal interview with the dean, if possible. If this is not feasible, for geographical reasons, the dean will often appoint a librarian in your area to conduct the interview and report to the school.
4. A reading knowledge of at least one foreign language (except for those planning to be children's or school librarians). One university states that a reading knowledge of both French and German is desirable for all students and particularly important for those interested in scholarly library work. In the past, this language requirement has proved to be a roadblock for some students. It can be met

after starting graduate work, but this means an investment of more time and money. So plan to take care of this requirement during your undergraduate years. It can usually be fulfilled by two years of one language or one year each of two languages. To be safe, however, check the catalog of the school you plan to attend.

5. Good health. Contrary to the stereotyped impression, work in a library—with some exceptions—is not sedentary. Librarians dealing directly with the public are extremely active—lifting heavy books, pulling and lifting catalog drawers, moving back and forth to the shelves. And they are on their feet more often than not during an average working day.

Furthermore, whether they are in direct contact with the public or not, most librarians these days work under considerable pressure. So you need a nervous system that can withstand considerable battering and—even more important—a philosophy of life that enables you to roll with the punches. In other words, you need physical and mental stamina.

Finally, looking ahead, you will probably have to pass a physical to get that first position. Not to mention the fact that most universities now require graduate students to take a physical on campus or to present a statement signed by the applicant's doctor.

This does not mean that there is no opportunity in the library world for people with physical handicaps. There is. A handicap does not necessarily mean poor health.

Library schools vary somewhat in the number of required credits. The average, however, is around 30 units of graduate courses, with some required and the remainder elective. Of course, a specified grade level must be maintained, usually a B average. Nearly all schools require a final comprehensive examination.

Accredited library schools require certain basic courses. Titles may vary from school to school, but the content is similar.

Reference Sources

Basic course, to acquaint you with the most commonly used tools; specialized bibliographic courses; humanities, social sciences, science.

Cataloging and Classification

Even though you do not plan to become a cataloger, you cannot function effectively in any library without a solid knowledge of how a library is organized and arranged.

Introduction to Librarianship

Development of the modern library and current trends; survey of library literature.

Administration

An introductory course; organization and management of different types of libraries. Even if you have no desire to become an administrator, you will need this information for day-to-day operations.

Selection of Materials

Criteria for building and maintaining collections; sources of information.

Depending upon your specialization, there will be additional requirements. For work with children, for example, one or more courses in juvenile literature and reading guidance; for special libraries, data processing and/or information on storage and retrieval.

Aside from these requirements, library schools vary greatly as to emphasis and course content because curriculums are changing. A campus supposedly reflects the society it serves. In reality, the tumultuous events of the 1960s revealed that in most cases it reflected and served only certain segments of American society. When the social upheaval in the city swept onto campus, it forced curriculum changes. The extent of such change has, of course, varied from institution to institution, from department to department. In some cases, change has been swift and drastic; in others, slow and timid. Where library schools are concerned, the speed and extent of change has differed. But change there has been—and doubtless there is more to come.

You will discover, for example, that some schools now require a course in data processing. Librarians of the future will be expected to be on speaking terms with the computer. Many library school catalogs list a course for future school librarians, The School Library as a Materials Center. Schools now offer courses or institutes dealing with the library's role in the changing social scene.

One of the most exciting experiments in library education of the 1960s was "High John." The name? High John was a mythical man whose cunning and wit could outfox the "Massa" of the antebellum era in the South. High John was a spokesman, a morale builder for the slaves.

The modern-day High John was born in October of 1967. Conceived by the School of Library and Information Services at the University of Maryland, it was a library in an urban slum (Fairmont Heights, Md.). It was also a laboratory, an educational experiment—hopefully, a pioneer. The project had a twofold objective: to provide service to a deprived area and to initiate change in library education.

High John broke almost every rule and regulation of a typical middle-class library. It was housed in a house— just a single-story house—on an unpaved back street in the midst of the community. Anyone could borrow a book—no geographical qualification and no ID were required (a card was mailed to the borrower's home, and if he received it that was considered sufficient ID). A parrot presided over the children's room.

The usual read-or-get-out edict went by the boards. High John was at times noisy. In the words of one project leader, "We can't allow the library to become a recreational center. We're a library. We don't need silence, but we do have to have a certain degree of quiet. Nor does everyone have to be reading all the time. Anyone can do anything he wants in the library, as long as he doesn't interfere with anyone else's freedom."

High John was a difficult, at times dangerous, experiment for the faculty and students. But the dean of the library school feels that it was a necessary experiment: "The university has been too disengaged, too detached. It belongs in this kind of social effort. And certainly a professional school has a commitment." (For a detailed account of High John see *Library Journal,* January 15, 1968.)

Library schools have begun to realize that the librarian who wants to work with unmotivated people must have special training. A bibliographer or a cataloguer needs his special skills. So does the librarian who is eager to wage war on illiteracy, cultural apathy and social injustice.

It is too soon to predict whether High John, and other bold experiments, will succeed. Such projects do indicate, however, that the wind of change is blowing through the library schools. In the case of the Maryland experiment, it became almost a gale; in other instances, it may be but a feeble breeze. What can be safely predicted is that changes are under way to make librarianship more relevant to our times.

The fact that library schools are changing is of crucial importance to you, the future library school student. It means that you should compare the catalogs of the various schools, to find the curriculum that best suits your interests. Investigate—thoroughly—before you invest your time and money, your energy and aspirations.

ADVANCED DEGREES

Ph.D. programs are on the increase in the library world. Such a degree will be an asset, in some cases a requirement, if you want to teach in a library school—a field, incidentally, where a severe shortage exists. The same will hold true for administrators in college and university libraries.

There is emerging a trend toward a second year of graduate study—after the master's, a year of concentration on a specialized field. At the end of the two years you will have the M.L.S., plus a certificate in your specialty.

Some schools favor one approach, some the other. So, again, check carefully.

FINANCIAL ASSISTANCE

Monetary assistance is increasingly available. Funds come from various sources: the library schools themselves, state library commissions, state and other library associations and private philanthropic foundations. And, recently, sizable sums have come from the Federal Government. As funds available vary from year to year, you will need to survey the situation when the time comes.

Sources for Up-to-Date Information

"Financial Assistance for Library Education," a publication listing scholarships and financial assistance for the academic year, provides a list of scholarships and grants administered through state library agencies, national and state library associations, associations of school librarians, A.L.A.-accredited library schools and other institutions offering graduate or undergraduate programs in library education. National associations, foundations and other agencies known to grant assistance for library education are also listed. Copies available from A.L.A., 50 E. Huron

Street, Chicago, Ill. 60611. One copy 50 cents. Or check with your public library.

Also in your public library, ask the librarian for pamphlet material on scholarships and occupations.

College catalogs. The annual announcements of all graduate schools include information on what financial assistance is available.

In addition to scholarships and fellowships, once you are in library school there are various work-study programs—trainee programs in cooperation with public libraries and research assistantships on campus. Again, library school catalogs will tell you what opportunities are available at a particular university.

The point is, do not think of lack of money as an insuperable roadblock. There are many sources for scholarships and fellowships, many ways to earn while you learn.

CHOOSING A LIBRARY SCHOOL

You will notice the accompanying list of "accredited" schools. In addition to these, there are more than a hundred colleges and/or universities with library education programs at the graduate level, and more than 200 offering undergraduate courses.

What is accreditation? It is the process by which an agency or an association (in this case A.L.A.) accords recognition to an educational institution that meets certain specified minimum standards. As of 1969 there were 39 accredited schools in the United States and three in Canada.

Accreditation is a valuable yardstick, but need not necessarily rule out an institution not listed. A private college, for example, may well have an acceptable program and a competent faculty but, lacking financial resources, will not meet the standards for the number of books in the library. What lack of accreditation does mean is that the prospective student should find out *why* that particular program has not been accredited.

Another thing to consider is the special emphasis or strength of the various schools. For example, the University of Illinois Demonstration Laboratory provides audiovisual services and equipment to students and faculty; the University of Texas has outstanding collections of original manuscripts and Latin American materials; Rutgers University offers courses in systems analysis, abstracting and indexing for information services and programming theory for information handling.

Cowles Guide to Graduate Schools includes an "Of Special Interest" section that provides some indication of special emphasis and strengths. But, again, you will get the clearest picture of the various schools by studying and comparing their catalogs. Large public and college libraries maintain collections of graduate school catalogs.

For general information, graduate and undergraduate, consult *American Universities and Colleges* and the *College Blue Book*.

XI

IF YOU'RE NOT A LIBRARIAN

Without the many people working in a library who are not librarians you could not get a library card, find a book on the shelves or take it out. And the same applies to audiovisual materials.

Information on nonprofessional positions is included for two reasons. First, if you enjoy libraries but do not plan on the years of college necessary for an M.L.S., there are still many opportunities open to you in the library world. Second, if you do plan on four or five years of college, these nonprofessional positions can help to finance those costly years.

The staff of a medium-size library or a specialized department, on the average, might consist of one senior librarian, five or six librarians, one children's librarian, one or two library assistants, five or six clerk typists, three or four clerks and five or six pages. There might or might not be a trainee and/or student worker.

A smaller branch, open to the public fewer hours and with a smaller collection to maintain, of course has less staff, but the ratio of professional to nonprofessional positions remains roughly the same. In other words, nonlibrarians outnumber librarians.

What do the nonprofessional members of the staff do? Library literature uses the phrase "supportive staff," meaning that the nonprofessional staff supports the work of the trained librarian. This is the theory. In practice, what does it mean in terms of specific jobs?

WHO DOES WHAT

Page (Also Known as Messenger Clerk)

A single patron may return two novels, one travel book, one how-to on interior decorating and six children's books. Multiply by X number of patrons, and the result equals your principal task—i.e., sorting and getting books back on the shelves in the right place. The same for pamphlets and magazines and audiovisual materials. In larger libraries, which maintain back files of magazines and newspapers, you fetch issues requested by patrons. In addition, there are workroom duties—reinforcing floppy magazine covers and lettering, to mention some random examples. You will be supervised by a librarian or library assistant. Contact with the public is limited.

You need strong feet and sturdy muscles, for you are on your feet most of the time and lifting constantly. Educational qualifications are minimal, but there may be other requirements. For a full-time job in a system operating under civil service you may have to pass an examination. Requirements vary, so drop into your nearest library and find out what they are in your particular community. One thing is essential—*accuracy*.

As nearly all public and campus libraries are open in

the late afternoon and early evening hours, they offer excellent opportunities for students in need of work. Many students, starting in high school and going on through graduate school, have helped to finance their education as full- or part-time library employees. And many librarians started out sorting and shelving books.

Clerical Staff

At the circulation desk you register new card holders, check materials in and out and handle reserves, renewals and overdues. The routines themselves can be memorized on the job or by following instructions as set forth in the office manual or as given by a librarian or library assistant. What cannot be memorized are attitudes for dealing with the public—a public which is usually pleasant, always unpredictable, sometimes difficult. In other words, you should enjoy working with and for people. However, a clerk or clerk-typist in a department of a large library, or a special library of whatever size, may work entirely behind the scenes (except, of course, at the circulation desk). So if you are hesitant about dealing with people, remember that there are many positions requiring little or no contact with the public.

Behind-the-scenes duties will vary, according to the size and type of library. They may include checking in new books and magazines or preparing books for bindery. They will undoubtedly include filing and maintaining records. Whatever your specific duties, you will work closely with a librarian or library assistant.

Until the coming of the computer a clerk-typist spent many hours typing overdue notices, but today the computer is beginning to take over such dull chores. Notice the word "beginning," for the library world is still in the early stages of adapting the computer to its needs. Once again, situations vary, and in your area overdue notices may be typed by human hand for a long time to come.

All of these duties, whether with the public or in the workroom, require *accuracy*. As to the computer, it requires more accuracy—not less. You may marvel at the speed of the print-outs. But remember that there first has to be an input—information that is fed to the computer by human beings. Remember also that the computer has no decision-making ability. So that if you, the human being, provide the wrong input, the computer will provide the wrong output. To take a specific example, the computer provides the Los Angeles Public Library with a book identification number—a BIN. If a library needs to replace or add a book to its collection, it is ordered by BIN. This greatly simplifies the ordering procedure, but if the number is wrong the library receives a book it does not want. Suppose the library wants BIN 085686—an archeology book. But the typist makes a mistake and types 085685—so the library gets a book about the old West. A wrong PIN—patron identification number—can create a public relations problem. One wrong digit and Jane Doe's $10 overdue notice goes to John Doe, who then storms into the library demanding an explanation.

Most libraries now use business machines, other than typewriters. A charge-out machine is so simple to operate that it can be mastered in a matter of minutes. Not so simple is changing the film in it—especially if a line of patrons is waiting impatiently. Larger libraries use cash registers to make change for overdues, etc. Copying machines are becoming commonplace, even in smaller libraries, and you may be called upon to show patrons how to use them. In a medium-size library with a switchboard, the clerical staff often doubles as PBX operator. Finally, with libraries in the process of being linked in networks, teletypes are making their appearance. You need not know how to operate any of these business machines before applying for a position, as you will be trained on the job.

Educational requirements vary, but usually include a high school diploma and/or the ability to pass a civil service examination.

You need reasonably good health and physical and emotional stamina, for you are under considerable pressure at peak periods. Patience and tact are essential if the job calls for working with the public.

As in the case of a page, you can work as a clerk or clerk-typist and continue your education. And with the increasing need for library assistants and/or technicians, the opportunity for advancement is growing.

Library Technical Assistant (Sometimes Called Library Technician or Library Aide)

A rose by any other name may smell as sweet, but an occupation with so many titles presents some thorny problems.

The confusion began some years back when the shortage of librarians became acute. A report in one of the professional journals put it bluntly: "Despite an increase in recruiting effort, it becomes ever clearer that the library schools will not produce enough professional librarians (at least for a very long time) to meet the vast and expanding need of librarians across the country."

In the past, what appears to be merely semantic confusion could have been brushed aside as absurd and unimportant. In the past, a person learned library procedures working as a clerk for several years, then took an examination and moved up to the better position—whatever its label.

Today, however, a new factor is being considered—educational requirements. Various proposals have been published, and are under consideration by the profession. It has been suggested, for example, that the library assistant position require a bachelor's degree (with or without a minor in library science). The technician or technical assistant will require some specialized training. This may be acquired, as before, on the job or—a recent trend—through formal courses at a junior college. There are currently about 100 community colleges offering degrees in library technology.

It must be emphasized that these are *proposals,* the pros and cons of which are still being debated. Since there exists no uniform, nationwide pattern, you will need to find out what the requirements are in your particular area. Regardless of the title and requirements, what it comes down to is this—these positions are subprofessional. That is, they are a separate and distinct classification, falling between the clerical and professional staff.

Perhaps the clearest description of the confused situation appeared in the December 1968 issue of *Occupational Outlook Quarterly.* Here, in part, is the explanation of what a library technician does and what training he or she needs.

Until recent years, the professional librarian was the sole custodian of the library's books and performed all the services related to their use. Today, the library technician performs many of the librarian's less skilled job functions. For example, the technician may furnish the public with information about library services; assist persons in locating books and other materials through the use of card catalogs and indexes; answer "ready reference" questions that require only brief consultation of a standard reference text.

Behind the scenes, library technicians may write simple descriptions of books—title, author, edition, publisher, publication date, and number of pages—for the card catalog. To order books and materials, technicians look up prices, publishers, and related information. Some technicians maintain files of newspaper clippings, photos, pamphlets; some arrange displays.

In a large library, technicians may be responsible for maintaining controls on checkouts, reserves, renewals, and overdue library materials. Often, a minor flair for mechanics is useful, for many technicians operate and maintain audiovisual equipment. . . .

A high school diploma or its equivalent is the standard minimum job entry requirement for library technicians. Most technicians presently employed have been trained through on-the-job training programs lasting 1 to 3 years. Recently, however, many new hires have been trained in formal post-high school programs—usually in junior or community colleges. In the future, formal training may become an entry requirement. . . .

Young people interested in a career as a library technician should be aware that the curriculum in a particular college is often tailored to meet the needs of local libraries and may not qualify students for jobs in libraries outside the immediate area. In planning their training, students should look into the requirements of libraries in the locality in which they want to work. Moreover, students who look forward to becoming professional librarians should be advised that credits earned in a 2-year college program in library technology are not necessarily applicable toward a professional degree in library science.

To this account might be added certain important personal qualifications:

> Initiative, tact and firmness—for supervising pages and/or clerical staff.

> Discretion, judgment and a friendly personality—for dealing with the public at the circulation and reference desks.

> An interest in information and how to find it—for helping at the reference desk. And the ability to say "I don't know" and summon help from the librarian.

> The ability to understand and follow directions, and to explain them to others.

> Awareness of need for accuracy and attention to details.

Trainees and Student Assistants

As previously mentioned, nearly all large libraries use student employees on an earn and learn basis. The duties of these temporary employees may include those of the clerical staff and/or of the library technician.

Book Repairers

The bindery departments of large libraries employ people to mend and repair materials, usually for the entire system. When pages are loose, torn or rumpled and when the spine is loose or breaking, materials are mended. If books are of only temporary value, if the paper is poor or margins are too narrow to permit rebinding, books are repaired. Book repairers also bind musical scores and pamphlets and reinforce maps, magazines and children's "easy" books.

Smaller libraries may also do their own rebinding, rather than send materials to a commercial binder.

If you enjoy working with your hands, investigate the bindery department.

NONLIBRARAIAN SPECIALTIES

Audiovisual Technicians

The more libraries make such materials available, the more technicians are needed. Both equipment and materials must be inspected and repaired. Especially for the multimedia centers in schools and colleges, electronics technicians are a necessity to keep all the hardware in working order.

Artists

Some of the larger public libraries employ their own artists and/or photographers for displays and publicity. As the multimedia centers of educational institutions develop, there will be a need for more graphic arts specialists. The graphic artist will produce transparencies and prepare materials for instructional TV; make charts, graphs, dioramas, etc.; and arrange displays, exhibits and bulletin boards. The photographic specialist will play an important role in the multimedia concept. Among other things, he will make films, TV shows, slides and filmstrips.

Public Relations

As libraries have grown larger and more complex, and as the communities they serve need more information and more services, the necessity for PR programs has become apparent. The PR expert on the staff of a large library acts primarily as a coordinator, supplying information to the various media. This may be on a large scale—for a bond issue or National Library Week activities. On a less spectacular scale, he may supply speakers for community groups or participants on radio or TV programs; he may plan a booklist based on, say, a forthcoming movie.

But who compiles the booklist? Who appears on TV or before a group? Who puts up the exhibits in the neighborhood branches? Answer: the librarians, usually. In the final analysis, the librarian is involved in public relations every moment he is in contact with the public. And not only the librarian, but every member of the staff who deals with the public. The PR expert builds on a foundation of goodwill and good service, and that foundation can only be laid by the people who work with the public.

FOR MORE INFORMATION

A.L.A. BULLETIN, April, 1968, and October, 1968.
Both issues include articles about subprofessional positions.

Baker, Priscilla Aubrey. "Library Technician," *Occupational Outlook Quarterly,* December, 1968.

XII

THE OCCUPATIONAL OUTLOOK

This is a world of bigness. The population is big. To provide food and products for it, business is big. To provide services, government bureaucracies are big. This is also, needless to say, a world of machines.

Some people feel comfortable with bigness, excited by miracle machines. Others do not. They do not want to spend their working hours encased in the impersonality of a big organization; they do not want to be a data-processed cog in a big machine. They *do* want to work for and with other human beings, and they want the opportunity to learn and grow while doing it.

Libraries are big, and growing bigger. Information science is making increasing use of machines. But the library world is still a place where you can choose the type of work which suits *you*—where you can be part of today's inescapable bigness, and still retain and develop your own particular individuality.

THE CHOICE IS YOURS

Types of Libraries

There are opportunities in:

Public libraries—from great metropolitan

systems, with hundreds of trained workers, to those in rural areas run by a single person

Government libraries, national and state

School libraries:

Elementary—increasing in number
Junior and senior high—with the developing multimedia centers

College libraries

University libraries—reference and research, with their many collections

Specialized libraries and information centers

Audiovisual collections.

Type of Work

There are opportunities for:

The generalist
The specialist
The nonprint enthusiast
The technologically minded
Working with the age group you most enjoy
Teaching in a library school.

Type of Temperament

There are opportunities for those who want:

Stability, but not stagnation

Adventure:

Jobs overseas

Jobs at home; librarians often work in
different types of libraries and in various parts of the country during their
careers

There are opportunities for those who are:

Introverts—librarians who procure and
process materials

Extroverts—librarians who work with the
public.

MONEY AND OTHER PRACTICAL MATTERS

Salaries

A shortage of librarians has brought about a sharp rise
in salaries. It is estimated that since 1950 the average
paycheck for beginning librarians has about doubled.
And because libraries are increasing in importance as
well as in number, salaries have continued to rise.

Salaries vary according to location and type of library.
Therefore you need to inquire about the current pay
scale in the area and type of library of most interest to
you. *The Occupational Outlook Handbook,* a government publication which will certainly be available in a
library near you, gives an indication of average earnings.
Also, the *Bowker Annual* gives average salaries for starting librarians.

Hours

Most public and college librarians work some evening
hours and Saturdays on a rotating basis. Campus li-

braries are usually open on Sundays, and there is a growing demand for Sunday service in public libraries.

Catalogers and other behind-the-scenes librarians keep regular business hours, as do special librarians in business, government, etc. School libraries usually follow the classroom schedule, but open earlier and close later.

Five-day workweek; 35 to 40 hours.

Vacations

They vary, depending on the policy of the individual library or the system within which it operates. Paid vacation after a year's service is usually two or three weeks, in some cases four. Vacations may be longer in school libraries (but remember that some of that time may be without a paycheck) and somewhat shorter in those operated by business and industry.

Fringe Benefits

Most librarians are covered by sick leave. Medical and group insurance plans, as well as a pension program, are offered by nearly all libraries.

Worthy of Note

Formerly the library world was thought of as almost exclusively feminine. This is no longer the case. As salaries rose to the point where men could support families on them, they have entered the profession in growing numbers. Many are in administrative positions or in the fields of science, business or technology. They are to be found, too, in the more traditional areas of the humanities. And there is a growing trend for men to work with young people.

For women the library world has certain unique assets. If they have children, they can frequently return to work part time when school age is reached, and to a full-time career when the children are grown.

Long before the phrase was coined, many libraries had been practicing "equal opportunity." In some corners of the library world, as in some corners of the country, the gate of discrimination still bars the door. But, for the most part, the door is open to anyone with the necessary qualifications.

Employment Outlook

There is no guarantee that you will find your ideal job immediately upon graduation from library school. However, the 1968-69 *Occupational Outlook Handbook* rated the employment outlook for librarians as "very favorable," with excellent opportunities in most parts of the country and in all types of libraries.

The handbook pinpointed some of the reasons for the "very favorable" situation: "The demand for fully qualified professional librarians to meet the requirements of a growing and increasingly well-educated population will be intensified by the vast and continuing expansion in the volume and variety of materials which must be processed for reader use. Also, because of the ever-increasing demands upon high-level executives in business and industry, management will rely more heavily on the services of special librarians and science information specialists to keep abreast of new developments. . . . Improved standards for school and college libraries and the expanding student population will also necessitate the employment of a growing number of fully trained librarians. Furthermore, as new methods of storing and retrieving information by means of computer equipment are developed, demand for science information specialists will be very great. . . ."

To put it another way, in a field that is growing, that is moving with changing technology and with changes in society, the opportunities are almost unlimited. The choice is yours.

FOR MORE INFORMATION

American Library Directory. New York: R. R. Bowker Company, annual.

Lists libraries in the United States and Canada; state school library agencies; library schools and courses; armed forces libraries and information centers overseas; index to educational institutions and special libraries. Available in large libraries.

Bowker Annual. New York: R. R. Bowker Company.

For up-to-date information. Salaries; Federal and state legislation affecting libraries; library schools; library trainee and student librarian programs.

Gates, Jean Key. *Introduction to Librarianship.* New York: McGraw-Hill, 1968. The library and its contribution to society; past and present, trends and problems of the future. All major aspects of this rapidly expanding field. See especially Chapter 24, "What of the Future?"

Library Literature
The "Reader's Guide" to library publications. An index covering all aspects of library and information science. Available in large libraries.

Occupational Outlook Handbook, prepared by the Bureau of Labor Statistics of the U.S. Department of Labor. (Revised every two years.) Describes the employment outlook, training requirements, earnings and working conditions in about 700 occupations.

Occupational Outlook Quarterly. Supplements the handbook with up-to-date, current developments.

Paradis, Adrian A. *You and the Next Decade.* New York: David McKay, 1965. Trends affecting careers in the 1970s.

For current information about a career as a librarian—salaries and educational requirements, accredited schools and scholarship assistance—write to:

> Office for Recruitment
> American Library Association
> 50 East Huron Street
> Chicago, Ill. 60611

PROFESSIONAL ASSOCIATIONS

Librarians work together in many organizations. Founded in 1876, the American Library Association is the oldest and largest. It is organized into *divisions,* each representing the interests of a type of library or a type of library work; *committees,* some permanent and some ad hoc; *round tables,* each established for a specific purpose (for example, Social Responsibilities Round Table —Information Science and Automation Division—Intellectual Freedom Committee).

In addition, there are associations for librarians in specialized fields and in the educational world. And, finally, states have organized their own associations: California Library Association and the like.

National associations include:

American Association of Law Libraries
American Association of School Librarians (division of A.L.A.)
American Library Association
American Theological Library Association
Association of American Library Schools (division of A.L.A.)
Association of College and Research Libraries
Catholic Library Association
Medical Library Association
Special Libraries Association.

For a complete list, statements of purpose and current addresses, see *Bowker Annual.*

PROFESSIONAL JOURNALS

The American Library Association publishes more than 20 periodicals and newsletters. And other associations also issue publications, on a regular or on a from-time-to-time basis.

American Libraries (formerly *A.L.A. Bulletin*), American Library Association.

Catholic Library World, Catholic Library Association.

College and Research Libraries, Association of Col-
lege and Research Libraries (division of A.L.A.).
Library Journal, R. R. Bowker Co.
Library Quarterly, University of Chicago Press.
Library Trends, University of Illinois Press.
School Libraries, American Association of School Li-
brarians (division of A.L.A.).
Special Libraries, Special Libraries Association.
Top of the News (for juvenile and young adult li-
brarians), American Library Association.
Wilson Library Bulletin, H. W. Wilson Co.

This list, by no means complete, represents the publications most readily available. Ask the librarian which
ones your library has.

GRADUATE LIBRARY SCHOOLS ACCREDITED BY THE AMERICAN LIBRARY ASSOCIATION

February 1968

Northeast

Catholic University of America,
Department of Library Science, Washington, D.C. 20017
Rev. James J. Kortendick, Head

*Columbia Universty,
School of Library Service, New York, New York 10027
Jack Dalton, Dean

Drexel Institute of Technology,
Graduate School of Library Science, Philadelphia,
Pennsylvania 19104. Kathryn Oller, Acting Dean

Unversity of Maryland,
School of Library and Information Services, College Park,
Maryland 20742. Paul Wasserman, Dean

State University of New York, Albany,
School of Library Science, Albany, New York 12203
John J. Farley, Dean

*University of Pittsburgh,
Graduate School of Library and Information Sciences,
Pittsburgh, Pennsylvania 15213
Harold Lancour, Dean

Pratt Institute,
Graduate Library School, Brooklyn, New York 11205
Louis D. Sass, Dean

*Rutgers University,
Graduate School of Library Service, New Brunswick,
New Jersey 08903. Neal Harlow, Dean

Simmons College,
School of Library Science, Boston, Massachusetts 02115
Kenneth R. Shaffer, Director

Syracuse University,
School of Library Science, Syracuse, New York 13210
Edward B. Montgomery, Dean

Southeast

Atlanta University,
School of Library Service, Atlanta, Georgia 30314
Mrs. Virginia Lacy Jones, Dean

Emory University,
Division of Librarianship, Atlanta, Georgia 30322
A. Venable Lawson, Director

Florida State University,
School of Library Science, Tallahassee, Florida 32306
Harold Goldstein, Dean

Universty of Kentucky,
Department of Library Science, Lexington, Kentucky 40506
Lawrence A. Allen, Chairman

Louisiana State University,
Library School, Baton Rouge, Louisiana 70803
Mrs. Florinell F. Morton, Director

University of North Carolina,
School of Library Science, Chapel Hill, North Carolina
27514. Walter A. Sedelow, Jr., Dean

George Peabody College for Teachers,
Peabody Library School, Nashville, Tennessee 37203
Edwin S. Gleaves, Director

Midwest

*Case Western Reserve University,
School of Library Science, Cleveland, Ohio 44106
Jesse H. Shera, Dean

*University of Chicago,
Graduate Library School, Chicago, Illinois 60637
Don R. Swanson, Dean

*University of Illinois,
Graduate School of Library Science, Urbana, Illinois 61801
Herbert Goldhor, Director

*Indiana University,
Graduate Library School, Bloomington, Indiana 47401
Bernard M. Fry, Dean

Kansas State Teachers College,
Department of Librarianship, Emporia, Kansas 66801
Robert Lee, Director

Kent State University,
School of Library Science, Kent, Ohio 44240
Guy A. Marco, Dean

***University of Michigan,**
Department of Library Science, Ann Arbor, Michigan 48104
Russell E. Bidlack, Acting Chairman

University of Minnesota,
Library School, Minneapolis, Minnesota 55455
David K. Berninghausen, Director

Rosary College,
Department of Library Science, River Forest, Illinois 60305
Sister M. Girolama McCusker, O.P., Director

Wayne State University,
Department of Library Science, Detroit, Michigan 48202
Robert E. Booth, Chairman

Western Michigan University,
Department of Librarianship, Kalamazoo, Michigan 49001
Jean Lowrie, Head

***University of Wisconsin,**
Library School, Madison, Wisconsin 53706
Margaret E. Monroe, Director

Southwest

North Texas State University,
Department of Library Service, Denton, Texas 76203
C. G. Sparks, Director

University of Oklahoma,
School of Library Science, Norman, Oklahoma 73069
Frank J. Bertalan, Director

University of Texas,
Graduate School of Library Science, Austin, Texas 78712
Robert R. Douglass, Director

Texas Woman's University,
School of Library Science, Denton, Texas 76204
D. Genevieve Dixon, Director

West

***University of California,**
School of Librarianship, Berkeley, California 94720
Raynard C. Swank, Dean

University of California, Los Angeles,
    Graduate School of Library Service, Los Angeles,
    California 90024. Andrew H. Horn, Dean

University of Denver,
    Graduate School of Librarianship, Denver, Colorado 80210
    Lucile Hatch, Acting Dean

University of Hawaii,
    Graduate School of Library Studies, Honolulu, Hawaii 96822
    Robert D. Stevens, Associate Dean

*University of Southern California,
    School of Library Science, University Park,
    Los Angeles, California 90007. Martha Boaz, Dean

University of Washington,
    School of Librarianship, Seattle, Washington 98105
    Irving Lieberman, Director

Canada

**University of British Columbia,
    School of Librarianship, Vancouver 8, B.C.
    Samuel Rothstein, Director

McGill University,
    Graduate School of Library Science, Montreal 25, Quebec
    Virginia E. Murray, Director

**University of Toronto,
    School of Library Science, Toronto 5, Ontario
    Brian Land, Director

---

* Offers program for doctoral degree.
** Basic program at the fifth-year level leads to the professional
bachelor's degree.

INDEX

Alcott, Bronson, 138
American Economic Review, 85
American Library Association, 31, 41, 45, 67, 72, 108, 139
American Library Directory, 114
American Universities and Colleges, 129
Army Library Program, 102
audiovisual departments, 71-78

Baldwin, James, 44
Billings, Dr. John Shaw, 23, 98
Bingham, Caleb, 58
bookbaggers, 62
bookmobiles, 78-82
Brady, Mathew B., 93
Braille books, 93
Bray, Rev. Thomas, 35
business libraries, 115-117

Carnegie, Andrew, 38-40, 112
Catcher in the Rye, The (Salinger), 64
Clark, Kenneth, 45, 47
Crabbe, Buster, 76

Department of State Library, 101

"Desiderata" (Ehrmann), 28
Directory of Occupational Titles, 122
Directory of Special Libraries and Information Centers, 114

ecology, 121
Edison, Thomas, 71
Ehrmann, Max, 28
Elementary and Secondary Education Act, 31
Emerson, Ralph Waldo, 97

federal libraries, 91-106
Federal Register Division, The, 98
Film Advisory Service, 72
filmstrips, 73
Fire From the Ashes: Voices of Watts (Schulberg), 44
Folger, Henry Clay, 113
Franklin, Benjamin, 36
Frost, Robert, 77

Go Tell It on the Mountain (Baldwin), 44
Government Organization Manual, 98

Guidelines and Standards for Public Library Service, 77
Gutenberg Bible, 93

Hamilton, Alexander, 93
Harvard, John, 127
Hentoff, Nat, 67-68
"High-John" experiment, 158-159
Higher Education Act, 31
Higher Education Facilities Act, 31
Hollerith, Herman, 22
Horn Book, 60
Humphrey, Hubert, 49
Huntington, Henry E., 112

I.L.L. (Inter Library Loan), 26
Images of the Future (Trump), 140
Index Medicus, 25, 99
Invaders From Mars, 76

Jefferson, Thomas, 93, 101
junior college library, 133-135

Kennedy, John F., 52-53, 54
Kim, 60

Lawes and Libertyes . . . of . . . Massachusetts, 113
librarian, the
    audiovisual services and, 71-78; bindery departments and, 88-89; bookmobiles and, 78-82; career preparation for, 149-162; catalog departments and, 86-87; children's books and, 58-63; circulation services and, 87-88; college libraries and, 127-137; definition of, 9-10; the disadvantaged and, 83-84; duties of, 9-17; education of, 149-162; federal libraries and, 91-106; National Archives and, 97-98; National Library of Agriculture and, 100; National Library of

Medicine and, 24-25, 98-100; non-professional careers and, 163-172; occupational outlook for, 173-181; order departments and, 84-86; public libraries and, 52-70, 71-90, 91-111; school libraries and, 138-148; social change and, 35-51; special libraries and, 112-126; state libraries and, 106-111; technological change and, 19-34; technical services of, 84-90; today's library and, 9-18; young adults and, 63-70
library aide, 167
Library of Congress, 24, 26, 29, 30, 36, 87, 91, 92-96, 107
Library Services and Construction Act, 31, 79, 110
library technical assistant, 167
Library War Service Program, 41
Lincoln, Abraham, 93, 97
Lindbergh, Charles, 94
Little Women, 60, 138

Mann, Horace, 139
MARC (Machine Readable Catalogue Data), 30
McCarthy, Joseph, 105
medical libraries, 117-119
MEDLARS (Medical Literature Analysis and Retrieval System), 24-25, 99
messenger clerk, 164
microrecorded materials, 72-73
Mr. William Shakespeares Comedies, Histories, & Tragedies, 113
Moore, Anne Carroll, 59
Morgan, J. P., 113
motion pictures, 72
Mumford, Quincy, 24

National Archives, 97-98
National Defense Education Act, 31

National Library of Agriculture, 100
National Library of Medicine, 24-25, 98-100, 117-119

Occupational Outlook Handbook, 16, 175, 177
oceanography, 121

page, 164
Paradise Lost, 113
Perry, Admiral, 97
picture collections, 73
Pilgrim's Progress, 113
Prophet, The (Gibran), 65
Public Library Demonstration Act, 108
Pychon, Thomas, 57

Raisin in the Sun, 76
recordings, 72
Research Centers Directory, 114

Salinger, J. D., 64
Sandburg, Carl, 77
Scan, 28
school library, 138-148
Schulberg, Budd, 44
Spenser, Edmund, 19
state libraries, 106-111
Statistical Abstract of the United States, 55, 129
Stevenson, Adlai, 28

Thoreau, Henry David, 97
Trump, J. Lloyd, 140

USIS, 103-104

V (Pychon), 57
Vanity Fair, 113
Viva Zapata, 76

Wright Brothers, 94

ABOUT THE AUTHOR

Vanya Oakes was born in Nutley, New Jersey; she received her elementary and high school education in Boston, Massachusetts. After graduation from the University of California at Berkeley, she set out to follow in the footsteps of her clipper ancestors and see the Orient. Her first book was an account of ten years as a journalist there. Upon her return to the United States she wrote a number of children's books, drawing upon her knowledge of the people and countries of the Far East. She also taught journalism and world affairs at Los Angeles College and began work on a Master's degree in Library Science at the University of Southern California. Since 1959 Miss Oakes has been a librarian with the Los Angeles Public Library, first in the Social Science Department and at present in the Hollywood Regional Branch Library where she is a reference and young adult librarian.